Other Books by

What Managers Need to Know

Productivity and Results

Performance Based Management

Rate Yourself as a Manager

You're in Charge: A Guide for Business and Personal Success

The Inside Advantage

Nobody Gets Rich Working for Somebody Else

Personal Performance Contracts

If They Can – You Can! Lessons from America's New Breed of Successful Entrepreneurs

Rate Your Executive Potential

Management Ideas That Work

How to Export: Everything You Need to Know to Get Started

Ready, Aim, HIRE! (Co-author)

The Entrepreneurial Family: How to Sustain the Vision and Value in Your Family Business

Family Ties and Business Binds: How to Solve the Inevitable Problems of Family Businesses

Think Like a Manager

Sleep Disorders: America's Hidden Nightmare

Sales Manager's High Performance Guide:
The Only Reference You Need to Build a Powerful Sales Force

A Team of Eagles

How to Manage Your Boss

The Small Business Troubleshooter

Wars of Succession

Fast Track: How to Gain and Keep Momentum

One Step Ahead: The Unused Keys to Success

Bounce Back and Win: What It Takes and How to Do It

Magnet People: Their Secrets and How to Learn From Them

Little Things – Big Results:
How Small Events Determine Our Fate

How to Make Your Boss Your Ally and Advocate

Building Your Legacy: One Decision at a Time

100 Ways to Bring Out Your Best

After You: Can Humble People Prevail?

Sharpen Your Competitive Edge

ON CD-ROM

The Personal Business Coach

Beyond Commitment: The Skills All Leaders Need

“Fact: Life is not guaranteed.
Question: If mine continues
tomorrow, what will I make of it?”

Nothing Ventured, Nothing Gained

Clearing the Way to Success

Roger Fritz

Inside Advantage Publications
Naperville, Illinois

Published by:

Inside Advantage Publications
1240 Iroquois Drive, Suite 406
Naperville, IL 60563
Phone: 630-420-7673
Fax: 630-420-7835
rfritz3800@aol.com
http:://www.rogerfritz.com

Unless specifically noted by name, all quotations are attributable to the author, Roger Fritz.

http://www.rogerfritz.com

Inside Advantage Publications
Naperville, Illinois

ISBN 1-893987-26-4

Reprinted Network Leadership South Africa (Pty) Ltd
P O Box 13541, Mowbray, 7705
This edition is not for distribution in or to bookstores

To Harold and Harriet Goddard,
my wife's parents,
who with no complaints
showed us what high standards
and hard work can accomplish.

INTRODUCTION

The older I get, the more I am convinced that the best advice I can give anyone, especially young people, can be expressed in three words:

Life Is Anticipation.

Yesterday is gone and will not return. Today is what I make it to be, but tomorrow depends on how I anticipate my options and prepare to deal with them.

The best test of this theory, I have found, is to visit a nursing home. Most residents there have little to look forward to except perhaps to stay alive. But even that motive does not appeal to some of them.

Anticipation keeps us going. Whether it involves fear or pleasure, exhaustion or rest, hard work or leisure, excitement or boredom, career or hobby . . .

We want to believe we have a future, and that it will be better.

This book was written to focus on what I believe is the key element of anticipation – Venturing. It concentrates on the most common "holdbacks" involved in overcoming fear and hesitation by offering specific ways to counter them. Suggestions are reinforced with real life examples and illustrations. My hope is that it will help enable you to find new ways to clear the way for your success.

Contents

CHAPTER 1

Opportunities Are Created, Not Given

> "Success is not found, it is made."

Probably the most distinguishing characteristic of Americans historically is that they have preferred to depend on themselves. Only recently have significant numbers seemed to prefer government initiatives for employment and "security." The record shows however, that freedom depends upon individual initiative and capitalism depends upon the creation of new forms of commerce and industry – beginning with small businesses.

Fortune favors those who help themselves because:

- Luck is not dependable.
- Necessity is the mother of invention.
- Venturing releases creative instincts and energy.
- Small organizations can change quickly.
- Individuals can experiment and control risks.

So what clues should we look for in finding self-starters? Here is my list:

Look for Kids Who:

- Can delay gratification
- Are less selfish
- Help their parents
- Can entertain themselves

Youth Who:

- Earn money on their own
- Save for their education
- Are not totally dependent on their parents after age 18
- Take pride in their appearance

Adults Who:

- See what needs to be done, and do it
- Seek responsibility
- Value their reputation
- Sacrifice for long-term goals

> "Success without failure comes only in dreams."

Luck Is Not Dependable

"When winning is an accident, don't count on it again."

Are some people just plain lucky? Maybe initially, but even if luck plays a part in their good fortune, what they do with that luck makes them a true winner. To depend on luck is a big mistake.

What you do with a given situation determines whether you win or lose. Sometimes realizing an opportunity will be your greatest challenge, but once you've identified an advantage, your true fortune depends on capitalizing on your ideas and being adaptable.

A good example of a lucky person who took advantage of his situation and made it profitable was W.K. Kellogg. Kellogg was experimenting with creating a healthier type of bread and left boiled wheat paste in a pan overnight. In the morning, he baked the dried out ingredients and ended up with toasted flakes. They were tasty and he decided to sell them as Kellogg's cereal. But his lucky accident wasn't the only reason for his success. His product was inexpensive to produce and naturally, other competitors entered the market.

At this point his product could have failed, but Kellogg decided to differentiate it from others in the market. He created the flakes out of corn and then added sugar. He also was one of the first to advertise heavily, especially to women, through such magazines as *Ladies' Home Journal*. He soon developed brand loyalty and his corn flakes led all his competitors. Kellogg took a mistake and created his own advantage.

George Richmond also took a good idea and made it great. Born into a single parent household in a poor New York tenement, he certainly qualified as "disadvantaged." But George was an artistic, inquisitive, hardworking, and optimistic child. Eventually, he was accepted to Yale University on a full scholarship. After he graduated, he became a schoolteacher in New York City.

In Richmond's classroom, he taught children from poor financial backgrounds like himself how to make money and how the economy works. Through games and simulations, he explained the basics of business such as banking, real estate, taxes, finance, and market demands. Bottom line: His programs became so successful he started a company called MicroSociety School, then sold the curriculum to 200 schools in 40 states, and helped thousands of children. He seemed like a lucky man whose good idea flourished. Not so. Life was never easy for Richmond.

At the age of 37 he was struck with Parkinson's disease and could no longer work. His business partner and wife had to take over the business. Was this the end for Richmond? Absolutely not! Even though he couldn't work at his business, he could still paint – a childhood passion. Now Richmond is a successful artist, selling some of his paintings to celebrities, including Muhammad Ali. George Richmond doesn't quit, he adapts.

> "Dependent people say 'It's lost,' confident people say, 'I'll find it.' "

Necessity – Mother of Invention

By simply solving your own problems, you can create new business opportunities. Chances are that someone else has the same problem and you'll have an immediate market. By finding a solution, you're not only helping yourself, but you're helping others.

Elisha Otis enjoyed solving problems. Does his name sound familiar? Next time you're in an elevator, look on the wall next to the door and you'll probably see his name the name of his company, Otis Elevator.

Raised on a farm, Otis did not like most of the work and spent most of his time trying to improve the family's equipment. Eventually he moved to New York and became a mechanic. He worked on many projects, always trying to invent a better product. If one idea failed, he'd move on to the next one.

Otis was especially interested in freight elevators. In the early 1850s he worked on making them safer and more practical. At the time, elevators were used to lift lumber or construction materials. If the rope broke, the materials in the elevator came crashing down. These accidents were costly, so Otis developed an elevator that would stop itself. Surprisingly, no one seemed impressed by his new invention so he decided to attract attention by demonstrating it at the 1854 New York World's Fair. Standing on an elevator lift, workmen hoisted him 30 feet above the ground. Dramatically, Otis cut the rope. The audience gasped, expecting him to fall to his death. But his invention stopped his fall and the orders poured in. In the year 2000, Otis Elevator had over $6 billion in sales.

> "Finding opportunity is easy;
> just look for mistakes."

During WWII and the Vietnam War, GIs had to solve their problems quickly and accurately. Their ingenuity saved their lives while fighting in the combat zones. For example, during WWII the Germans put metal piano wires across the roads to decapitate GIs who were driving along unsuspectingly in their jeeps. When others heard about this gruesome tactic, it didn't take long for the Americans to modify their vehicles with metal poles. The poles snapped the wires before they encountered the traps.

In Vietnam, many were killed and wounded when shrapnel from land mines exploded underneath their vehicles. Solution: place sandbags on the floor of the trucks and jeeps. It worked. Rocket-propelled grenades presented another problem. Answer: put hurricane fencing around the vehicles, creating a cage. Miraculously, the grenades would bounce off and hit the ground. Adaptability and necessity saved many lives. These solutions were so effective that they were used on Humvees during the Gulf War.

> "The most significant trait of losers is they don't recognize opportunity."

Venturing Releases Creative Instincts and Energy

Venturing into new territories or directions is challenging, but the rewards can be great. Most of the time we don't like change and are more comfortable with what we know. But forcing yourself to leave your comfort zone can be worthwhile and profitable. Growth and improvement come only if we continue to learn by observing our environment, asking questions, and studying new ideas. Successful people are lifelong learners. They want as much knowledge as they can get to improve their lives and are always curious.

Thomas Jefferson set a high standard for all of us. He took notes on his daily observations. Every morning he spent hours writing and researching his ideas.

He wrote observations when he traveled abroad and brought that information back to the United States. He also detailed the small things in his life, like how well certain plants grew and the type of seeds he used. He was always experimenting.

Jefferson believed idleness was his enemy. In a letter to his daughter, he said crisply, "It is wonderful how much may be done, if we are always doing." Jefferson's heritage is unsurpassed. He wrote our Declaration of Independence in 1776, was elected the third U.S. president in 1801, and founded the University of Virginia in 1825.

> "Be thankful for what you don't know.
> Only in discovery will you find opportunity."

Venturing solves problems and creates new opportunities. James Naismith's innovative thinking led to a sport that is enjoyed by more than 300 million people worldwide.

In the late 19th century, football was dangerous and sometimes deadly. Athletes didn't wear helmets or safety equipment. Naismith was an athlete who was discouraged from playing football by his friends and family, but wanted to be involved in sports all year round.

As a physical education teacher, he was ordered to find an indoor game for a class of rowdy students at the School for Christian Workers in Springfield,

Massachusetts. First, he tried bringing lacrosse and soccer inside. That didn't work. So he decided to try something completely new and without as much physical contact. He found a medium size rubber ball, nailed a bottomless peach basket to a wall and called the new game Basketball.

In his lifetime, Naismith didn't spend a lot of time coaching, but tried to bring sports into young people's lives. He believed athletics helped teach goal setting, ethics and teamwork. He also stressed safety and made the first football helmet. Many people believe his concerns about safety and physical conditioning influenced the specialty of sports medicine. The Naismith Memorial Basketball Hall of Fame in Springfield Massachusetts honors his legacy.

> "Leaders are always scanning and sorting for the next breakthrough ideas."

Small Organizations Can Change Quickly

In America you're free to choose your type of education, employment, career, and develop your own opportunities. With hard work, you can build on your ideas and talents. In many countries, career options are still dependent upon social or economic status. If your father was a rice farmer, you'll be a rice farmer, without considering your personal desires, interests or skills.

It's always exciting to see a person with a new idea succeed beyond their dreams. Bob Page was an auditor during the day, but on weekends enjoyed collecting china and crystal. In 1981 he decided to extend his hobby. He hired a part-time assistant and opened a business he called Replacements, Ltd. The concept was that he could find a match and complete set of china, crystal, or silver, even though the pattern was no longer being manufactured. In his first year, Page sold $150,000 worth of merchandise. Three years later, sales reached $4 million and in 2002, totals over $69 million.

Currently, Replacements, Ltd. has over 10 million pieces in inventory and a 300,000 square foot warehouse, the size of five football fields. It is now the largest supplier of china, crystal, silver and collectibles. Amazing!

Elaine Hodgson, President and CEO of Incredible Technologies has seen her company grow at an astounding rate. In the early 1980s she helped design one of the first digitized computer games. In 1985, Hodgson and a co-worker Richard Ditton decided to start their own business. They called it Incredible Technologies and used their $150,000 to create an interactive coin-operated video golf game, Golden Tee Fore!

In less than ten years, the company sold more than 100,000 machines and became a $65 million dollar privately held business. Today it is one of the largest US designer and manufacturer of coin-operated video games.

> "In America nobody says you have to keep the circumstances somebody else gives you."
> – Amy Tan, writer

Sometimes success and growth come from unexpected places. Father Bernard McCoy was in charge of the temporal needs and activities of the Cistercian Abbey in Wisconsin. He was buying toner cartridges for the monastery's printers, but couldn't believe the retail markups of 1000 to 2000 percent! McCoy decided to contact the manufacturers directly in hopes of getting a reduced rate for his monastery. In fact, he wondered why not sell them at a lower cost to other non-profit organizations as well?

Several producers liked his idea of selling and encouraged him to sell directly to non-profit organizations as well as businesses. McCoy agreed, and with the volunteer help of a California public relations firm, LaserMonks.com was born.

The abbey is now self-supporting and the monks saw their sales grow from $2000 in 2002 to over a half-million in 2003. Sales are expected to exceed 1.5 million in 2004. Father McCoy found a winner.

Individuals Can Experiment and Control Risks

> Successful people believe they have had many opportunities.
> Losers believe all of them were stolen.

Even though taking a chance is frightening, it doesn't have to be uncontrolled. You can experiment with a new idea or venture and still be in charge of your risks. That's the purpose of business incubators!

They are designed to help start-up companies or emerging businesses to control their costs and share the resources. Usually located in older manufacturing buildings or industrial parks, they offer shared or below-market costs of equipment, technologies, rent, and support services, such as accounting and marketing. Many are designed around a specialty such as manufacturing, technology, or healthcare.

In 2001, the National Business Incubation Association reported that incubators provided assistance to over 35,000 startups which created 82,000 full-time jobs. The total number of business incubators has expanded from only twelve in 1980 to over 950 in 2003.

Tim Lavengood, Executive Director of the Technology Innovations center at Northwestern University, believes that a poor economy has little effect on incubators. It may be harder for start-ups to find financing, and some stay longer in incubators, but it is very encouraging to note that new business isn't affected as much as an existing business by downturns.

In a poor economy, many of those forced out of their jobs decide to start new businesses. The Fulton Carroll Center in Chicago houses individuals who are starting businesses as diverse as piano repair, bread makers, metal workers and flower designers. Owners can rent space from as large as 20,000 square feet to an area as small as 8 by 10 feet. It gives new businesses a place to set up immediately with office space, a connection to a telephone, heat, and air conditioning, plus the support and services needed for it to get going. Success rates are going up because they have more control over risk.

"Winning without preparation is luck. Only fools depend on luck."

Michael Powell's father, Walter, liked to compare business with fishing. Walter taught his son that a fisherman only made money when his line was in the water. Young Powell took his dad's advice and opened a bookstore with $3,000 while he was a University of Chicago political science student. One summer, Walter worked with Michael and enjoyed the experience so much he returned to Portland to open his own bookstore. In 1971, Michael Powell's lease was up so he joined his father in Portland.

Walter Powell had a novel idea at the time to sell both used and new books at the same store. Michael was hesitant at first, but the idea was a great success. From the beginning, Powell's Books treated customers courteously and paid them a fair price for their books.

The store's reputation grew as well as its profits. In 1997, they opened an online store, and in 2003, 35% of the company's sales were from the online business.

Powell is convinced that it's important to find out what large companies aren't doing, or aren't doing well, because that means opportunity. "The only people I see who ever make it are the ones who find the cracks," says Michael.

But instead of going head to head against their largest competitors, Powell's Books worked with them. Even though Amazon took away some new book sales, they adapted and concentrated on used and out-of-print books. Now, Amazon uses Powell's for used and rare selections and they have about 1,000 partnerships with other companies. They are constantly increasing profits by looking for new markets, such as adding textbooks. Powell's has seven locations in the Portland area and more than a million books available.

Lessons: by starting out with a minimum investment and staying adaptable, the Powell's have demonstrated that experimenting with low risk ideas can be very profitable and provide outstanding growth.

Chapter 2

The Poison Pills

> "Resolve is never enough.
> We must begin."

I have never known anyone who was lucky for a long time. "Breaks" come and go, but lasting benefits require sustained effort. Winning without preparation is luck. But the temptations to wait for good things to happen can be very powerful. I call them poison pills because when we yield to them, they are deadly.

They are:

1. Waiting for Inspiration
2. Waiting for Approval
3. Waiting for Perfect Timing
4. Waiting for Guarantees/Assurance
5. Waiting for Support
6. Waiting for Security

Let's consider how each can prevent progress.

Waiting for Inspiration

> "Beware of those who can work and don't; they are toxic"

Ideas Die without Effort

Most of us are not like J.K. Rowling, now a very rich author. While writing the Harry Potter story, she was on living on public assistance, divorced, and had a baby daughter to support. "The story idea for 'Harry' just fell into my head while riding on a long train journey," she says. J.K. wrote in a small café everyday with her child beside her for five years. Who could have imagined Rowling would win The British Children's Book of the Year Award, and earn her millions in the American movie industry! Encouragement is nice but it never gets the job done.

Joni Eareckson Tada, founder and president of Joni and Friends, is a world-wide symbol of persistence. Just like "Superman" Christopher Reeves, her quadriplegic disability didn't prevent Joni from success and inspiring millions. She has proved that some people's only disability is waiting to be inspired.

As a teenager, Joni was paralyzed from the neck down after a diving accident. She loved art and for hours painfully taught herself how to paint by using an elongated brush placed between her teeth. Her paintings were described as amazing and breathtaking. But this remarkable woman didn't stop there. She went on to write a book about her life simply titled *Joni.* Her book was made into a motion picture and translated into fifteen languages.

Joni was appointed to The National Council on Disability and served three and a half years. In 1979 she found Joni and Friends, an organization that ministers to the disabled. In 2002, Joni and Friends served over 500 special needs families at nine family retreats, collected and refurbished over 14,000 wheelchairs, and produced a daily five-minute radio show broadcasted by 850 radio stations. Now you tell me – is Joni disabled?

> "Neither a wise man nor a brave man lies down on the tracks of history to wait for the train of the future to run over him."
> – Dwight D. Eisenhower

Most people who know Irving Berlin's songs are shocked to learn he grew up a poor Russian Jewish immigrant in the New York City tenements. From that humble beginning he created over 1000 songs, including "Alexander's Ragtime Band," "White Christmas" and "God Bless America," plus many successful Broadway musicals. The youngest of eight children, he earned his own money by age 14 from singing in New York City's Lower East Side Bowery Saloons. His composing career began when he discovered writing songs earned more money than singing.

> "The worst times makes for the greatest opportunities."

Success didn't come easily to him, and he lived to watch his influence decline. Berlin learned to live with many setbacks. When praised by a fan's remark, "I'll bet there is no one who has written as many hits as you have," he replied, "I know there is no one who has also written so many failures."

> "The more I practice, the luckier I get."
> – Gary Player, Golfer

In 1981, Grant Tinker became the chairman and chief executive of NBC when the Network ranked in last place. But he is credited by many for saving NBC in the 80s by increasing the quality of television. Tinker, who produced his wife's "Mary Tyler Moore Show," believed in hiring the best producers, writers and creative staff. His leadership earned NBC shows more Emmy Awards than ABC and CBS combined.

> "The most difficult part of getting to the top of the ladder is getting through the crowd at the bottom."
> – Arch Ward, Sports Writer

Tinker believed in giving the best shows the necessary time to find an audience, instead of immediately canceling those with lower ratings. He felt that by providing quality programming, the audience would find them and he was right. By the mid 1980s, NBC, was the number one network with hits like "Cheers," "The Cosby Show," "Hill Street Blues," "Night Court," and "St. Elsewhere."

Waiting for Approval

> "Ideas in the head are common, but nothing changes until they are brought into action."

Whose approval are you waiting for? Are you expecting the nod to go ahead from parents, spouse, friends, or employer? That may be the worst thing you can do. Fanny Blankers-Koen, named as the best female athlete of the 20th Century by the International

Athletic Federation, didn't need approval. They said she was too old at age 30 to compete for the Netherlands in the 1948 London Olympics. During her prime, she missed the 1940 and 1944 Olympics because of World War II. In spite of the fear of Nazi occupation, and childbirth, Fanny continued to train and it paid off.

She left the 1948 London Olympics setting 20 world records, and winning four gold medals! Newspapers called her a poor mother for leaving two children at home. Shedding tears in the locker room, Fanny had to make a decision. She missed her children terribly, and had overcome other setbacks, but now everyone was against her. They called Fanny the "Flying Housewife." Her modest response was "All I've ever done is run fast. I don't see why people make a fuss about something I love to do."

> "A man cannot be comfortable without his own approval"
> – Mark Twain

Waiting for Perfect Timing

"The least understood cause for failure is indifference. Never begun, never done"

While working in a hospital, Bonnie Hunt once told a cancer patient how upset she was to be moving to California to try an acting career. "Don't worry about it," she said, "I wish I had time to fail." If you're waiting for perfect timing, you might as well quit today. There are always reasons *not* to do something. You can't start your diet today, because of a party tomorrow. You can't start a hobby, until you're retired. Blaming work, weather, money, spouses, bosses – the list goes on and on. Stop making excuses and apply the Nike commercial maxim: "Just Do It"!

Adam Witty didn't wait for the economy to improve before he started his company, Advantage Networks, which sells tickets online and does marketing at sporting events. In fact, he believes there can be advantages. For example, when the unemployment rate is high:

1) Hiring is easier.
2) Employees with better qualifications are available.
3) Wages are lower due to competition.
4) Rental space costs less.
5) Competition might be weaker because of their cost cutting.

The payoff? Chevrolet hired Witty to promote their brands at major league baseball games.

Sports Illustrated calls Roger Bannister's record in the mile run "One of the most important athletic accomplishments of the twentieth century." Why was he selected? Because he constantly analyzed his performance. He knew what he had to do to improve. In the 1952 Olympics, Bannister finished fourth and didn't receive a medal, but set a new goal – become the first to run a mile under four minutes. On May 6, 1954, even though there was a 65-mph crosswind and track conditions were far from perfect, he achieved his goal and startled the world.

Angel Munoz realized that computer gamers wouldn't always want to play in an isolated environment. In 1997 he started Cyberathlete Professional League, a company that sponsors computer gamer contests. Angel began setting up tournaments around the country. Many wanted to take advantage of his innovative idea but he was going to not let someone else pass him by. Leaving his job as an investment banker paid off. Each year more than 3000 Cyber Athletes compete in 30 countries.

Look around. Those who quit rarely get to the top. Consider these famous authors, for example. Pearl S. Buck, Pulitzer Prize winner, *The Good Earth*, was returned fourteen times. Mary Higgins Clark had her first book rejected forty times before finally selling it. Louis L'Amour had 200 rejections. Jack London had 600 publishers and agents turn him down.

Waiting for Guarantees/Assurance

> "The two worst enemies of progress are starting too soon and not starting at all."

Sometimes you simply have to make your guarantees. When Betty Fox was let go by her employer, she wondered what to do next. At 68, another job would be hard to land, and she didn't have computer skills or much knowledge about the Internet at the time. Despite this, Fox went on to create an extensive website for older people: GrandmaBetty.com. She did this from a small apartment with only her son for assistance.

GrandmaBetty.com catalogs links to sites older Americans are interested in through a comprehensive database. It also has forums, chat areas, reviews, and community information. She runs the entire site from a basic Internet account, with no server. Her book, *When One Door Closes, Another Opens,* discusses how Fox went from knowing little about cyberspace to managing one of the most successful sites in her niche – without employees or overhead!

Samuel Houston went from an aimless and contentious youth who battled alcohol to the one Southern Governor that refused to swear an oath to the Confederacy, even though it resulted in his removal from office. It is thought that Houston might have held more public offices than anyone in American history before him. While in the Army, Houston read the *Bible, The Iliad,* and other works while in the field or at garrison. He finished an 18-month Law program in 6 months. Sam Houston will be remembered as one of the few people that understood Santa Anna and as a tireless defender of Texas. "A nation divided against itself cannot stand," was a motto of his.

Waiting for Support

> "If we did all the things we are capable of doing, we would literally astonish ourselves."
> – Thomas Edison

There are exceptions, of course. Doris Drucker, the 80+ year-old wife of business guru Peter Drucker, decided she would start a business with the specific goal of selling it. Her children, she says, "thought I had 'gone off my rocker' " when she elected to prove that seniors could be entrepreneurs.

Her product is an electronic device that visually displays sound levels so a public speaker's volume can be tested quickly and accurately in an auditorium. It took her and her partner two years to get up and running as her husband, Peter, watched amazed. When asked if she would start another business, her answer was: "Yes, but I still have a long way to go with this one."

Waiting for Security

> "We qualify ourselves for a better future by doing things we are not sure we could."

"Personally, I never understood why progress should crawl when it can be made to leap," stated Walter Chrysler. The maxim served Chrysler well throughout his life. After becoming vice president of General Motors and president of Buick, he decided to found another car company instead of staying with GM. At first called Maxwell Motor Corp., their first car was the Chrysler, which was designed to provide as much quality as possible for a low price. The name was soon changed to Chrysler Corp. after their success. "The real secret of success is enthusiasm. I feel sorry for the person who can't get excited about his work," he said regarding his career. Sometimes you must create your own security, regardless of the competition.

Avoiding inaction and defeating pessimism is the only way to avoid the pitfalls of "security." Settling for the illusion of safety can cost you opportunities for a long time – perhaps even an entire career, if not careful. A study at Carnegie Mellon University charted the success of students that negotiate salaries and their perceptions of the process. 78% of the students who negotiated were able to increase their starting salaries by 7.4% (over $4,000, on average). Those who were overcautious were 30% more likely to fail at raising their compensation. You have to take the initiative; the world can't be yours without a first step.

Lesson: Bounce back and Win!

Never, Never, Never Give up"
– Winston Churchill

Chapter 3

The Antidotes for Doubt

"Doubt and fear are our worst enemies."
– William Wrigley, Jr. Executive

Doubt and uncertainty affects us all – no exceptions. Since perfection is unlikely, how do we avoid inertia? How do we get moving when we are standing still? We can:

- Wait to be rescued.
- Hope someone will see our problem.
- Hope someone will solve our problem for us.
- Trust our survival instincts.
- Study "what ifs" in advance.
- Keep moving forward.

In this chapter, we focus on the last two of these: life-long curiosity and unyielding effort, which builds confidence and self-assurance. The stories in this chapter illustrate very reliable advice:

1) Relentless Study Pays Off
2) Know the Territory
3) Keep Pushing for the Change You Want
4) Never Ignore the Facts
5) Share Your Ideas
6) Avoid Diversions
7) Seek Difficult Assignments
8) Don't Wait for Permission
9) Chip Away at Uncertainty
10) Character Counts
11) Start Early – Stay Late

Relentless Study Pays Off

> "The first step to failing is to doubt your ability. The last is to stop trying."

Air Force Col. John Boyd was a military strategist and an accomplished fighter pilot. Today U.S. pilots use many of his aerial warfare techniques. In 1997, he died at the age of 70. His biographer, Robert Coram, says, "Boyd is the most influential military thinker since Sun Tzu wrote *The Art of War* 2,400 years ago." Boyd grew up in Erie, PA. During his teens, after his father died, he worked three jobs to support his mother and four siblings. At the age of 18, he joined the Army Air Corps. His goal was to fly. After two years, he left the Army to get an economics degree and joined the Air Force ROTC at the University of Iowa.

Boyd had a hunger to learn. To perfect his piloting and training techniques, he studied calculus and engineering. A former Commandant of the Marine Corps said Boyd had an "unrelenting love of study." Sometimes Boyd's drive for perfection upset his superiors. If he thought the Pentagon's top brass was not concerned enough about having working systems adaptable for combat situations he was known to get into shouting matches which almost led to two court-martial proceedings. "He was more concerned about improvements in the military than the advancement of his own rank," says Coram.

After leaving the Air Force in 1975, he spent the rest of his career working as a private military contractor. An expert in air combat and engineering, Boyd become familiar with every known military philosopher and the different tactics used in hundreds of battles. He gathered the common characteristics and patterns that the winners of those battles shared and used this knowledge to form his own military strategies.

Although he caused a stir among the military, he also had many supporters. He was an effective communicator but not always tactful. Despite being blunt, or maybe because of it, Boyd gathered a large network of knowledgeable employees and colleagues over the years who helped him find ways to improve the armed forces. People respected his integrity and work ethic.

Know the Territory

> "The most effective leaders accomplish two things:
> • they outsmart critics
> • they improve the lives of their followers."

While Adam Samrah and his neighbor, Clyde, were having lunch, some friends called to tell him that a fire had started about four miles away from them down the mountain. The caller told Samrah that the fire was under control. By 4:00 in the afternoon, though, the wind changed. A sheriff's deputy drove by and told him to "Get out now!" Samrah started for his pickup but then wondered if his friend, Clyde, who lived across a shared pond, had heard about the danger.

Clyde and Adam tried to leave the area in their vehicles but walls of fire chased them back to Samrah's cabin. In minutes, Clyde's cabin was consumed by fire. The two walked to the center of the pond, hoping that the water would save them. The pond was only about 15 by 20 feet wide and three feet deep. They thought they were going to die and prayed.

All of a sudden, the smoke thinned. They ventured out of the water, which, for over eight hours, had protected them from the fire. The burn line circled Adam's property – ash on one side, undisturbed forest on the other. His house was fine. There was only one problem: his front door was locked. The friends walked down to the melted truck. They poked around through some ashes and found Adam's key ring. All but one key were melted or charred and misshaped. The one key? The key to his cabin. Luck? Maybe. Fate? Maybe. But one thing is certain – they know the territory.

Keep Pushing for the Change You Want

Few of us work for one year on a personal goal, but Susan B. Anthony kept working relentlessly on getting women the right to vote for *over 42 years*! Instead of waiting for something to change or to continue struggling to change the laws, Anthony decided one day in 1872 that she would "just do it." She and 15 other women voted.

Although the men working at the election site let the women vote, the local press demanded that they be prosecuted. Anthony was arrested. After posting bail, she lectured across the country for three weeks to gather support for her cause. Though she didn't live to see the Constitution amended to give women the right to vote, her devotion, conviction, and courage to stand up to injustice motivated the changes that led to the 19th Amendment.

> "Winners take action.
> Losers take their time."

R.V. Jones knew how to talk to his superiors – even when his ideas were rather unusual. Jones thought that he could "blind" German radar systems in WWII by having lead bombers drop strips of tinfoil. Although some thought the strips would get caught in the bomber's intake valves, after carefully providing the crews with instruction, Jones' idea was implemented and worked! The allies lost only 50 % of the aircraft previously destroyed on these missions. For this and other jamming techniques, Jones was given the Medal of Freedom in 1946. In 1993, the Central Intelligence Agency created an award in his name.

Never Ignore the Facts

> "One accurate measurement is worth a thousand expert opinions."
> – Grace Murray Hopper, Admiral, U.S. Navy

Charles Darwin was not someone most would have expected to be thought a leader. After being expelled from his local school in England because of poor grades and failing at becoming a medical doctor (he hated the sight of blood), he fell into a position as a naturalist on a ship, the H.M.S. *Beagle*. Despite being constantly ill, Darwin signed on for a five-year journey. He had to pay his own way and after his father refused to help, an uncle provided the money.

He collected specimens by walking, climbing, paddling, and hiking through rivers and jungles. Then, he dragged what the ship's captain called "useless junk" aboard for later analysis. He kept detailed notes about the weather, plants, animals, and people he observed throughout his journeys.

Because Darwin realized how unpopular his theories would be to religious leaders and others who believed in divine creation, he kept them to himself for more than 20 years. Then he gathered and presented the facts in his book *On the Origin of Species.* It became one of the most important ever published and still sparks debates today.

Share Your Ideas

> "Full potential is never found without overcoming the doubters."

Dave Longaberger believed that by sharing your dream, it more easily becomes reality. He had four main reasons:

- By sharing your dream, others can join you to work together to make it a reality.
- By sharing your dream, you can learn from other people's experience and expertise. They can give you feedback to help fine tune your dream.

- By sharing your dream, you make a commitment to it. Other people can help keep you motivated by asking you about progress.
- By sharing your dream, you make it a goal – a priority.

To prove his convictions, in 1973, Longaberger founded the country's leading basket-weaving firm with direct sales associates. In 2000, one year after his death, the company had 70,000 sales associates and $1 billion in sales.

Avoid Diversions

> "Accept life and you must accept some regret."
> – Henri Frederich Amiel, Swiss Philospher

At six, Neil Armstrong took his first airplane ride and started teaching himself about flying. He created a wind tunnel in his basement to test the crude aircraft he designed and built. As a teen, he paid for his own flying lessons by working after-school jobs and saving his money. By 16, Armstrong earned his pilot's license.

Still trying to learn more about flight, he joined the Navy in 1947. When the Korean War started, he became the youngest fighter pilot in his squadron. After the war, he earned his degree in aeronautical engineering at Purdue. Armstrong, a humble and private man, was famous for remaining cool under pressure, using logic and creative thinking based on knowledge to handle a crisis. When, for example, a thruster rocket short-circuited in a 1966 mission, he stabilized the craft and was later able to make an emergency landing in the Pacific Ocean.

It was no surprise to people who knew him that he was selected by the National Aeronautics and Space Administration as a crew member for the first moon landing. Millions watched his first step and heard the now famous words, "That's one small step for man, one giant leap for mankind."

> "The will must be greater than the skill"
> – Muhammad Ali, Boxer

His parents were nationally rated tennis players but they only introduced Ivan Lendle to the sport that became the love of his life. It was Ivan who pushed himself, practicing and playing all the time. He credits mental and physical conditioning as the keys to his success.

Lendle set specific performance objectives so he could have tangible evidence of his success. When he uncovered a weakness in his game, he would set aside three-hour workouts to correct his performance. When he retired in 1994, Lendle had won $21,282,417 in tennis prize money. He won 94 singles titles, second only to Jimmy Connor's 109. In 2001, Lendle was inducted into the International Tennis Hall of Fame.

Seek Difficult Assignments

> "To be an achiever, you must
> first believe you can.
> Do not listen to those who
> say you can't."

When Mildred Ella "Babe" Didrikson wanted to do something, she gave it her all. Her sister Lillie said that when Babe was learning how to play golf, "she hit and hit the ball until she had to put tape over her hands but she wouldn't stop." In 1933, Babe began to study golf seriously. She took golf lessons daily and hit 1,500 balls a day. She won the U.S. Women's Open golf championship three times (1948, 1950, and 1954) and was named to the Ladies Golf Hall of Fame. And that was after she was named All-American in basketball three times in a row, from 1930-1932.

Babe was named by the Associated Press (AP), Female Athlete of the Year six times (1931, 1945, 1946, 1947, 1950, and 1954) and was named the AP Female Athlete of the first half of the 20th Century. Not only did she excel in basketball and golf, she also won gold medals in javelin and 80-meter hurdles, and a silver medal for the high jump at the 1932 Olympics.

She faced her health and athletic challenges the same way. In 1953, doctors said her colon cancer was inoperable and had spread to her lymph nodes. They told her she would never play golf again. Fourteen weeks later, she entered a tournament and the next year won her third U.S. Women's Open.

> "If you have convictions,
> you will also have doubts."

Don't Wait for Permission

Maybe it was because his father died when he was only 4 years old . . . or because he had to leave school at the end of eighth grade . . . or maybe something else drove Glenn Curtiss to succeed. Curtiss took over a bicycle store in 1900 when he was in his early 20s. At his shop, he designed his own bicycle. Curtiss had, as they say now, a "need for speed" and an innovative mind. He soon attached a motor to the bikes.

After testing some purchased motors, he decided he could build one better himself. He opened a motorcycle shop and was soon selling his new bikes throughout the U.S., New Zealand and South Africa. Curtiss began racing motorcycles and set many land speed records. In 1907, his V-8 motorcycle raced 137 miles an hour and he became the fastest man on earth.

Convinced aviation was the future, Curtis started building airplanes. He believed a loyal workforce was the key to success, so he worked alongside his employees as a teammate. Even when he was a millionaire and lived far away from the plant he was known to send checks to those who were sick. He also continued to develop bigger and better planes, including an airmail plane, the famous WWI trainer, the Jenny, and the first front-wheel drive car.

Ricky Henderson stole 130 bases in 1982 – still the single-season record. But speed isn't his secret. "The biggest thing in stealing bases is not being afraid to get thrown out," he says. "Being able to put your full attention to your work is the key to success. Dedicate yourself to something that you want to improve in each and every day. Success is based on your work habits. Work hard each and every day." Henderson played Major League Baseball for 25 seasons. He was named the American League's Most Valuable Player in 1990 and played on World Series championship teams in 1989 and 1993.

Chip Away at Uncertainty

> "Doubts diminish us.
> Enthusiasm enables us."

Charlotte St. Martin thought a new property offered her company, Loews Hotels, an excellent growth opportunity. She was so certain she moved a manager and his family across country to start the new hotel.

Before they could close the deal, a buyer made moves to acquire the property. She told her newly relocated manager she'd keep him informed and that, if the deal fell through, she'd find him another opportunity within the company. The deal fell through and she kept her promise. By taking responsibility for her actions and keeping her employee informed, St. Martin won over her team.

Mark Tarner, president, Sound Bend Chocolate Co., agrees. "I like to give updates as information trickles in. If you're silent and you let things build up, people feel more directionless. Giving frequent reports on unfolding developments is in itself a great way to lead."

Character Counts

Over 12,000 high school students in 2002 were asked if they cheated at least once. 74% of them said yes. In 1992, 61% said yes. 38% admitted they had stolen something (compared to 33% in 1992) and 92% said they had lied to a parent. Almost half (43%) of the students said that they would lie to get a good job. Ironically, 75% of the students surveyed thought that they had high personal virtue.

One hiring manager, Sunny Kobe Cook, co-founder and former chief executive of Sleep Country, U.S.A., has found a way to see beyond a potential employee's slick presentation. "They best way is to observe them when they don't realize they're being watched," Cook says. She has applicants sit in the waiting area for at least ten minutes. During this time, the receptionist observes applicants' behavior. Does the applicant talk to or ignore the receptionist? Does the applicant show an interest in the company by asking questions or reviewing company materials displayed in the lobby? Oftentimes, Cook says, those 10 minutes in the reception area reveal as much or more about the true character of the applicant than the formal interview.

Start Early – Stay Late

> "Excuse is spelled 'if only'. Courage is gained only when we don't give in to weakness."

Many gymnasts would give up after trying a routine that ended with them falling into the judges' table, but Paul Hamm isn't typical. Somehow, he was able to shake off this horrendous mistake and continue. His performance won him the all-around gold medal in men's gymnastics in the 2004 Olympics.

Here's how he analyzed the situation: "I knew my mistake was costly, but I also still believed there was a possibility I could win a medal." Hamm's next two events were the parallel bars and the high bar. His nearly flawless performance earned him top scores and pushed him toward the gold.

Doug Stibel, one of Hamm's coaches, "He had the goal of showing the world what he could do and did not let one day go by without working toward it." Bo Morris, the men's program manager for U.S. Gymnastics put it this way: "Perseverance, hard work and determination. These are all the clichés you hear about to succeed. But in Paul's case, they are all true." So, beyond the inspiration of the "small town boy makes good" stories, there lies a simple truth –

> "Success comes only to those who believe in themselves and are prepared."

CHAPTER 4

Is Hunger Enough?

By far, the most reliable keys to success in venturing into the unknown are calculated risk and relentless effort. Short bursts of activity are usually wasteful if the energy cannot be sustained. We have all had those moments when we recognize we had a good idea that someone else implemented. The hurt is compounded if they made money doing it!

The same feelings result when we wonder how some "average" people get top rewards. Do they work harder to get opportunities or are they more enthusiastic about their work? The answers are not mysterious and begin to be revealed when we examine these six key issues:

- What successful people don't do
- Failure is temporary
- No regrets
- Just fix it
- Don't look back
- Find positive thinkers

What Successful People Don't Do

> "Successful people learn by doing. Their leaders have learned by doing *a lot*."

Successful people don't:

- Dwell on past mistakes.
- Seek to place blame.
- Procrastinate.
- Avoid accountability.
- Shoot the messengers of bad news.
- Exploit others for personal gain.
- Concentrate all authority at the top.
- Ignore the facts.
- Trust their instincts exclusively without counsel.
- Defend the present situation too long.
- Allow temper to cloud their judgment.
- Mistake status symbols, high incomes, and control over people and resources for leaders.

Dr. Charles Kelman is a versatile man. An ophthalmologist, saxophonist, and helicopter pilot, he holds 150 patents. He has received the American Achievement Award (a previous recipient was the inventor of the polio vaccine, Dr. Jonas Salk), and the National Medal of Technology (from the first President Bush).

How is it possible to become distinguished in such a variety of fields? Kelman's answer: focus, effort, and recognizing opportunity. Years ago, a friend gave him a short book entitled *It Works.* The book suggests writing down life goals and reading them at least three times a day. At first, Kelman had 40 goals, but he pared them down to 10. Among them were: a breakthrough in the medical field, professional success with his music, and becoming a helicopter pilot.

He soon discovered that the subconscious mind is powerful. Shortly after he wrote down his goals, he happened to see an issue of *Look* magazine discussing Dr. Irving Cooper's method of curing some neurological diseases by freezing the part of the brain causing the disease. When the proper part of the brain is frozen, the disease is cured. Kelman was certain he could use this freezing method to remove cataracts. First discovered in 1978, the technique is still widely used today.

> "The sun has not caught me in bed in 50 years."
> – Thomas Jefferson.

Thirty-five year old Tony Hawks, a legend in skateboarding for 20 years, knows about hard work and determination. Most people thought that a skateboarding trick, called a 900, which features an aerial two and a half revolution spin off a ramp was impossible. But after six years, a broken rib, and a back injury, Hawks felt confident enough to attempt it. In 1999, at the Summer X Games in San Francisco, he first successfully showed off his stunt.

Obviously, Hawks is committed to practicing. But he also talks about a commitment that happens in his mind before even attempting a trick. "Basically, once you commit to it, you're either going to make it or you're going to get hurt. There's not a whole lot of gray area there," he says. It's kind of like the rings on the school playground. At one point, you have a hand on each ring, but at some point, you have to let go of the ring behind you and move forward. You have to commit to the next step.

Hawks started skateboarding at 9, began competing at 11, turned pro at 14, and was the world's best by 16. Although he believes others have had more natural ability, he credits hard work, determination, and giving 110% to his success. Also, success nourishes success. The expectations of his fans motivate him to constant improvement and growth. In skateboarding circles, Hawks is credited with inventing over 80 tricks.

Since the Summer X Games in 1999, Hawks has parlayed his successes on the skateboard to very successful business ventures including a video game series, a line of sports clothing and accessories, kid's toys, and snack food. By keeping aware of the ever-changing youth culture, raising the bar for himself, working hard and remaining true to his down-to-earth, nice guy image, Hawks plans on staying successful.

"Every action has a consequence"

In the 1920s, when most book publishers were white Protestants, two Jewish men, one a piano salesman and the other a journalist, decided they wanted to enter this field. The pair's first project was a collection of crossword puzzles published in the *New York Sunday World*. The print run was 3,600 copies. The book came with a pencil and sold for $1.35. But soon, they had to hire 20 clerks to handle orders and by the end of the year they had sold almost 1 million copies.

By focusing on customer service – for both the reader and the bookseller – Richard L. "Dick" Simon and M. Lincoln "Max" Schuster started an innovative trend in book publishing. In 1925, they changed the industry by letting booksellers return unsold books for credit. Readers repeatedly confirmed Simon and Schuster's taste in books by purchasing the ones they selected.

Also in the mid 1920s, Simon and Schuster published a then expensive ($5.00) volume, *The Story of Philosophy*, by Will Durant. Again breaking the mold in the publication industry, the two spent up to 10 times more than their competitors on a marketing campaign. It worked.

In the late 1930s, focusing on a different segment of the reading market, they started a low-priced imprint they called Pocket Books. The paperbacks sold for 25 cents and were very successful. After the death of Franklin Roosevelt, in 1945, the team stunned the publishing world by releasing a book on the President's life only six days later. Now, Simon and Schuster publishes more than 2,000 titles a year, under 35 imprints. The founders' vision has been validated by 54 Pulitzer Prizes and a world-wide customer base.

Failure Is Temporary

> "The first step to career success is to recognize what you do best. The second is to nurture it."

As a child, Tennessee Williams loved to listen to stories. His nurse, Ozzie, told wonderful tales and his mother read him Dickens and Shakespeare. His father, a traveling salesman, told him stories about the importance of truth and honesty. Williams became addicted to the power and color of language.

At 11, Williams received his first typewriter. From then on, he had started a routine of writing a few pages every day. His father didn't like the idea of his son trying to make a living from a creative endeavor. But Williams vowed he would get paid for his writing, and he tried everything. As a teenager, he wrote for and sold a horror story to a pulp magazine. Later, he wrote poetry, short stories, essays, letters, plays, and novels.

In the 1940s, Williams pitched a screenplay to Metro-Goldwyn-Mayer. They rejected it, so he did some rewriting and changed the script for the theatre. The play, *The Glass Menagerie,* was produced in Chicago. The cast didn't believe in the script and started showing up for rehearsals late and drunk. Despite other people's opinions, Williams believed in the script. On December 26, 1944, the play opened to rave reviews. It was also well received in New York and won Best Play of 1945 from the New York Drama Critics' Circle.

Tennessee Williams had the self-confidence to believe that failure is temporary. He knew how to evaluate criticism and implement changes to improve his work. He knew how to turn failure into success.

"Failure is just another word for incubation."

In the 1880s, photography was not for amateurs. Cameras were heavy and bulky. To take a photograph, the camera had to be placed on a tripod. This meant someone had to lug a tripod to the location. Delicate glass plates were used to capture the image. Taking a photograph was an ordeal. George Eastman wanted to streamline the wet plate process to make his own life easier. Later, he realized that if photography were easier, many more people would be interested in taking pictures.

Although young Eastman made more than three times the average salary in his time, he wanted to start his own business. His goal: make the creation of high-quality photographs something everyone could do. For two years, he rushed home after work and experimented – sometimes from three in the afternoon until breakfast. Often tempted to give up, he kept going.

Then, in 1880, he started a business, Eastman Dry Plate Co., which changed photography forever. His company saved time and money by automating a process that had been purely manual. In 1888, Eastman announced a light-weight camera that could be used without a tripod. The Kodak sold for $25.00. Its price and ease of use increased the popularity of photography and brought Eastman closer to his goal.

When he introduced a transparent film, it became the new standard for capturing photographic images and Thomas Edison used this concept in the creation of motion pictures. Later, Eastman introduced color film and home movie cameras and photography became available to anyone, anywhere, anytime.

> "Successful people think of fear as excitement."

Heinrich Englehard Steinweg's life was filled with challenges. Born in Germany in the late 1700s, he was the youngest of 12 children. During the Napoleonic Wars, young Henry lost his mother and eight of his brothers and sisters. In 1812, while his father and the remaining four children lived in a small hut, their home was struck by lighting. Only Heinrich lived. Then 15, he survived by doing odd jobs until, three years later, he joined the army, where he learned woodworking and cabinetmaking. Heinrich found he loved working with wood and began making mandolins, dulcimers, and zithers.

After leaving the military, Steinweg worked at an organ company where he became fascinated with pianos. After studying their construction, he experimented with different woods, the cut of the keyboard, the action, and stringing of the instrument.

Soon he developed a cast-iron frame enabling him to put greater tension on the strings. Turning his theories turned into reality, Steinweg created a piano which produced a fuller better sound and enabled performers to use a wider dynamic range.

Steinweg's marriage produced six sons who all became involved in building pianos. By 1836, he, with his sons' help, had completed his first grand piano and two of his square pianos took a gold medal at the 1839 Brunswick State Fair. The Duke of Brunswick purchased the first grand piano and demand for his instrument increased.

In his small workshop, Steinweg and his sons were able to build up to 10 pianos a year. Then, the political scene in Germany changed. Recession settled in and piano sales dropped. Thinking that life would be better in the United States, he moved his family and business to New York City. During the day Steinweg worked in a piano factory and his sons worked in cabinetry shops. At night, the Steinwegs built and sold pianos.

Sensing growing anti-German feelings, Steinweg changed his name to Henry Engelhard Steinway. Their creative ideas were acknowledged by a medal at the London Exposition. In 1864, demand became so great, that they had to open a new factory. Business was booming. Then, in 1865, the Steinway family lost two sons: one to tuberculosis and one to typhoid fever. While still recovering from that loss, labor unrest at the piano factory ended in a strike. Somehow, the family pulled together again. Realizing that people with smaller homes also wanted great sounding pianos, Steinway introduced the upright. It had many of the same features of the grand piano but the strings were strung vertically, enabling the pianist to create a large sound on an instrument that takes up much less space. They too became popular and Steinway received 11 patents for his innovations for them. No doubt about it, Henry Steinway had indeed created his own future.

> **"Stay prepared so that your next idea will be your best"**

Not all exciting innovations come quickly. Allied-Signal, now merged with Honeywell Inc., kept working on a 50-year-old challenge: how can polyethylene be made into a super fiber? A few believed, because of its dense molecular structure, it could be turned into a "super" product that would be very useful and profitable.

Two scientists at Allied's research and development facility found a way. By converting the polyethylene into a gel before turning it into a fiber, they discovered the polymer could be spun into ultra strong strands. Allied called the new fiber Spectra. It was 10 times stronger than steel but light enough to float.

At first, the product was used for marine ropes and sails. Later, tests discovered the fiber could stop bullets. In the 1980s, Spectra was used to make bullet-proof body armor for police departments. This use expanded into the military market. Now, U.S. troops in Iraq and Afghanistan wear bullet-proof products made from the newest version of Spectra. Countless lives will be saved because of the persistence of a few "stubborn" researchers.

No Regrets

> "I've never known anyone to be successful if all they do is blame."
> – Marla Runyan,
> U.S. National Running Champion

Running in any competition requires rigorous training. But try to imagine running when you can't see objects directly in front of you. Marla Runyan faces this challenge every day. At age 9, she was diagnosed with Stargardt's disease, the leading cause of blindness in the U.S. Legally blind, she has learned to run by using her peripheral vision to guide her. Not only has Runyan learned to run, she excels. She has set the American indoor record for 5,000 meters.

Because she takes personal responsibility for her performance and gives all she has, Runyan believes that she can compete against the best runners in the world. Raised in a family that values self-reliance and ethics, she wants to do her best so she will have no regrets. To remind herself of this, she prepares for every race by repeating "No regrets, no regrets," to herself at the starting line.

Runyan's mother taught her that while people cannot control what happens to them, they can control their *reaction* to what happens. "I've never known anyone to be successful if all they do is blame. I think the secret to achieving something is holding yourself accountable for your choices, good or bad, and learning from your mistakes." she says.

> **"Winners focus not on what they have done, but what they have left to do."**

Lt. Gen. Ricardo Sanchez is the nation's highest-ranking Hispanic officer, but he has never forgotten his roots. Born second of six children, Sanchez was raised in a two-bedroom home by a single parent, his mother. Although the home had no running water, Sanchez says of his upbringing, "It was very basic living, a good environment for family values. It taught you a lot of discipline, a lot of perseverance, and also made you a little ambitious." While the

Sanchez children were going to school during the day, their mother went to school at night. She valued education highly and lived her values.

Whenever people told Sanchez he couldn't do something, he took it as a challenge. His high school counselor wanted him to be a welder like his father but, with the help of a professor, Sanchez received a four-year Army-Air Force scholarship to Texas A&I College, (now Texas A&M University-Kingsville), where he earned a BA in mathematics and history. Although he was told few ROTC officers got into the 82nd Airborne Division, and even fewer Hispanics, he did. For over 17 years he didn't see another Hispanic officer. He became a role model for minorities because he firmly believes in self-development. Determination to meet challenges head on has helped Sanchez rise from a battalion commander in the Gulf war to the nation's highest-ranking Hispanic. He is now a commander of coalition ground forces in Iraq. The job, which he sees as part military tactician, part politician, part businessman, and part social worker, suits him well.

> "Good intentions are not only hollow, they are deceptive when we are counted upon and don't deliver."

After working for one company for 25 years, Bill Erhart's life suddenly changed. Erhart, who went with Lucent Technologies when AT&T spilt up, thought he was stepping up to a new opportunity. Then he was laid off. Health insurance costs took off, his pension disappeared, and the family's savings were reduced. His wife, Pam, found work so the Erharts were able to make ends meet.

No one is happy about being unemployed, but Bill looked at it philosophically: "Globalization is a done thing. It's not going to go back. Jobs are going to continue to be exported . . . it's just a mechanism for the transfer of wealth from the 'have' countries to the 'have-not' countries," he says.

In the meantime, his wife advised those who had been laid off to be resourceful and flexible. Don't be locked into one field. Have a broad base of experience. Being laid off might give you the time to reconsider talents and skills that you haven't used for a while. You might find happiness and opportunities using these forgotten talents.

> "With a good partner, you can have eyes in the back of your head"

Layoffs affect the whole family. With the time a person needs to find new work increasing, and the feeling of loss of self-worth, many job seekers and their spouses find anxiety intensifies over time. Many couples struggle with role reversals, anger, and loss of self-esteem. Kathy Goulet learned this the hard way when her husband was laid off. After a while, Goulet felt her friends were growing frustrated because they didn't know what to say about her situation. She didn't want to burden her husband because she felt he was under enough stress.

Goulet and a friend, Michelle Plummer, decided to do something about this growing problem. They started a group, "Networking for Partners of Job Seekers," to provide a safe place for partners to support each other. The group educates attendees by inviting guest speakers to talk on a variety of subjects including health care benefits and starting a new business. Partners can also explore their feelings about their changing life situation. Every success story sparks a new one.

Just Fix It

> "Initiative begins in the mind,
> but cannot stay there.
> It is revealed only in action."

A well-known manager in a car factory once said, "The surest way to failure is to have everyone do exactly as they are told." The lesson is if employees do not feel their ideas are valued, they will only follow instructions. If they fear making mistakes, they will take no risks. But successful people and companies realize that everyone needs to feel they won't be fired for making a small mistake, and that problem-solving abilities should be encouraged.

Walt Disney knew this. He wanted to encourage his creative staff because he needed them to bring life to his ideas. To prove it, in the late 1920s, Disney paid his creative staff more than he earned himself. In the 1930s, to help them improve their ability to draw animals, he created a small zoo on the property. Later, he developed a generous bonus system to reward talent.

Wal-Mart founder Sam Walton invited his employees to implement change. If they found that something in the store wasn't working, they were to "just fix it." If the change solved the problem, employees were encouraged to share their solution with the rest of the store/chain. The now famous Wal-Mart greeter was one store manager's fix for shoplifting. By welcoming people to Wal-Mart, honest people feel welcome; dishonest people learn that someone is at the door watching them come and go.

The 3M Company encourages innovation in another way. It has an additional commandment: "Thou shall not kill a new product idea." If someone wants to stop a new idea, that person must prove the new product isn't feasible. The 11th commandment gives creative people the space to voice and develop new ideas without receiving unsupported negative feedback.

> "Creativity is the sudden cessation of stupidity."
> – Edwin Land, Inventor of the Polaroid camera.

Years ago, Cathy Hughes lost her apartment and car. She slept on the floor of her radio station while raising a son. She and her then husband had borrowed a million dollars to acquire a small radio station, WOL. The stress of the large debt crushed the marriage but Hughes kept sight of her dream.

With her skills on the air, WOL became profitable. In 1987, Hughes bought a second radio station. Now, she has 68 radio stations and a new cable station. Today, Hughes, 57, is worth about $300 million. Her son, Alfred, now 39, says, "My mother had a vision to do something and her mantra is that if you can believe it and conceive it, you can achieve it."

"We can't change the past.
Only the future can be altered . . .
<u>if</u> we are prepared."

Tired of living from paycheck to paycheck and being a self-described couch potato, Karen Young decided to auction off some household items and knickknacks on the Internet. Business picked up. She soon realized that packaging costs were eating into her profits.

After thinking about the Internet sales trade, she knew she couldn't be the only person with this problem. So, she called a manufacturer of bubble wrap and started having 740-ft roles delivered to her. She then began selling the bubble wrap in 50-ft. lengths on eBay for $2.95. This year her company,

ShippingSupply.com, will bring in close to one million dollars in sales.

Don't Look Back

> "Success comes less from inspiration than controlling negative thoughts."

While studying for his marketing degree, Aaron Driben worked at a courier business that served Washington, D.C., New York City, and Boston. Even though he was just a part-time worker, Driben noticed an opportunity. To prepare himself, he learned the business inside and out. Starting as a courier and moving into operations and sales.

After graduating from George Washington University, Driben convinced two people to invest in his new business, a same-day delivery service that would serve Boston. They saw Driben's intra-day delivery service as a counterpart to their overnight service. City Express, Driben's company, turned a profit in only four months. After two years, annual revenue exceeded $1.5 million. Over the past 13 years, sales have grown more than 1,000%.

Driben believes his success is due to meeting commitments, hard work, and a "customer-first" mentality. Many of his current customers have been disappointed by other services that promised delivery by a certain time but didn't meet the deadline. He negotiates a realistic delivery time and is open 24 hours a day, seven days a week.

> "Aim to be rich and you will find money. Aim to be useful/needed, and you will find success."

Steven and Patricia Williams had good jobs when the term "downsizing" started being used. Concerned about stability, first Stephen and then Patricia left their corporate jobs to start their own franchise. They selected Maids International Inc. Today, they have 35 employees. Some of their people have been with them for 10 years. In addition to having the financial security they wanted, Patricia says, "We're still learning every day. It wouldn't be fun otherwise."

Bruce Martin worked for the Chicago Board of Options Exchange for 22 years when he noticed that technology was taking more brokerage jobs. Concerned about his future, he started researching business opportunities. He, too, selected Maids International Inc. Although he expects he won't be able to draw a salary for a year, he believes that by keeping his customers and employees happy, the new life he has chosen for himself and his family will bring him the security he seeks.

Find Positive Thinkers

> "Success is based on your work habits each and every day."
> – Rickey Henderson, Baseball's all-time leader in stolen bases and runs scored.

For over 20 years, Lew Frankfort has been in leadership roles at Coach Inc. He's made mistakes but he has learned from them. In fact, Frankfort believes the best managers are those who have had successes *and* failures. "I am driven in part by a blend of striving for excellence and the fear of failure," he explains. His motivation and goals are passed along to employees and expressed in Coach's products because Frankfort hires people who are drawn to a high-performance culture. Their achievements then become the new standard for future performance. Constant improvement by people who are energetic, enthusiastic and positive thinkers makes Coach Inc. a very successful business.

Integrity and a strong work ethic are values the company demonstrates with its customers. Because Coach wants to build long-lasting relationships with its customers, if any Coach handbag needs to be repaired, the company does it free. Coach encourages partnerships and collaboration. Frankfort, however, is aware of differences among people and responds to them individually. If people are good at what they are doing, he gives them freedom to do their job. If people need some help, he becomes a teacher.

"To get better answers, unchain all seekers."

William A. Patterson worked for United Airlines nearly 40 years. During this time, United became one of the country's biggest and most successful airlines. Many attribute his success to the way he valued employees. When Boeing Air Transport, which later became United Airlines, purchased a competitor, someone wanted him to terminate many of the employees. "The personnel," he said, "are three quarters of the airline's assets." He found positions for almost all of the employees whose jobs were in jeopardy.

When Patterson believed in an idea, he saw it through to fruition. In the 1930s, flying was a new and frightening experience for many. One of Patterson's associates thought that having young women on board as crew members would have a positive, calming psychological effect on the passengers. Patterson added flight attendants to the crew.

To eliminate fear of air travel, Patterson gave wives of businessmen free trips so they could travel with their husbands. He was sure that the women would see that flights were safe and wouldn't worry so much about their traveling husbands. Patterson also believed in airline safety. At the time, the industry paid pilots by the miles they flew, which gave them the incentive to fly in risky weather. He changed this by guaranteeing pilots a minimum salary and offered a bonus to those who canceled flights in bad weather conditions.

The bottom line – in building United Airlines, Patterson took risks, but they were well-considered and calculated. He studied opportunities thoroughly and in many cases, avoided losses other airlines incurred because they didn't do the research or think far enough into the future.

> "To grow your business, bury your ego. Don't be the star. Be the star maker."
> – Bud Hadfield, Executive

CHAPTER 5

Survive or Thrive?

> "An Amazon tribesman is ignorant of many things, but in matters of survival is more alert than you and me. If not, he would surely be dead tomorrow. The question is, do we want to thrive or merely survive?"

The most significant difference between those who thrive or just survive is what I like to call **constructive compulsion**. Thriving requires:

- Facing facts first.
- Working when hurt.
- Objective projection of consequences.
- Self-confidence based on actual accomplishment, not daydreams.
- Careful analysis of the motives of nay-sayers.
- Realistic evaluation of barriers.
- Elimination of distractions.

Let's take a closer look at each:

Facing Facts First

> "Trailblazers do not wait for detailed instructions."

When he got home after taking a walk, George de Mestral, a Swiss engineer, found cockleburs all over his clothes. Instead of just being annoyed from pulling the burrs off the clothes, he was intrigued. Using a microscope, he noticed each burr was actually like thousands of tiny hooks that would grip thread, fibers, or animal fur. Looking closer, he discovered how the hooks were shaped and positioned to stick to any fabric or fur they touched.

After over eight years of research, Mestral perfected his new fabric fastener. He quit his engineering job, took out a $150,000 loan, found the best materials and designed the machine to create his new product. The company he started now sells more than 60 million yards of **Velcro** every year.

Working When Hurt

"Bet on those who have survived and against those who have surrendered."

Truett Cathy might have given up after any number of tragedies struck. But he kept his businesses going. His first fast food restaurant was opened in 1946, when Truett and his brother, Ben, opened a place called The Dwarf Grill in Atlanta. The Dwarf was a profitable venture almost immediately. But after only three years, Ben and another brother were killed in a small plane crash.

Truett worked hard to buy out his sister-in-law's share of the business. He did it in one year. Another year passed and a second restaurant opened. Shortly after doing becoming profitable, it burned down. Cathy had almost no insurance so rebuilding was his financial responsibility. During this time, his doctors discovered that he had colon polyps, which required surgery and extended treatment. Rebuilding the business was put on a back burner.

While recovering, he had an idea for a new sandwich. He would take a boneless chicken breast, season it, fry it, and put it on a bun. That product started the Chick-Fil-A chain, which today has 1,100 restaurants and sales of over $1.4 billion.

> "Talent plays a part, but mostly we are what we make ourselves become."

Born prematurely, Billie Lee Shoemaker wasn't expected to survive the first night. But the tiny two-pound infant pulled through, surprising everyone. Shoemaker grew to only 4 feet 11 inches and weighed under 100 pounds, nevertheless he loved athletics and in high school tried out for football, basketball, boxing, and wrestling. He was always passed over.

A classmate suggested that because of his size, he would make a good jockey. Although he loved horses, until then he hadn't thought about combining his two loves – horses and athletics. Young Bill began working as a barn hand and exercise rider. He watched other jockeys and learned from them. "I knew it took two, maybe three years before a kid like me would get the feel of riding, but I was willing to put in my time," he said.

The little man faced many challenges. He lost a lot of races and suffered several injuries, including a pelvis broken in five places, a ruptured bladder, and a paralyzed leg. But his positive attitude helped him recover and kept him going. At one point, he had not won a race in 21 years. People thought he was through. Then, at age 54, riding a horse others found unimpressive, he won his fourth Kentucky Derby.

But the worst was yet to come. Shoemaker was in an automobile accident leaving him paralyzed from the neck down. He learned to use a mouth-controlled wheelchair and continued training horses to ensure his daughter got through school. His career lasted 42 years. He won 8,833 races and made more that $120 million. Little body, big man!

"Survivors find ways to make pain a positive influence in their lives."

"Failure is a learning experience. If you learn a billion-dollar lesson from a million-dollar flop, it's a cheap education," says the co-founder of Amway, Rich DeVos.

DeVos and his high school buddy Jay VanAndel tried several ventures. The team's first business was Wolverine Air Service. Even though neither could fly, they bought a second-hand Piper Cub and soon had a fleet of planes. Using the profits from selling Wolverine, the two then purchased a Nova Scotia schooner to sail to South America. The boat sank.

They also tried importing wood carvings to the U.S., ran an ice cream shop, and had a rocking-chair factory. Each lasted only a short time. Finally, in 1959, they started Amway (short for "the American way of life") which sold a cleaner called Frisk. Amway is now a subsidiary of Alticar, which had $4.6 billion in sales in 2002.

Objective Projection of Consequences

> "Survival requires only a heartbeat. Success requires using all of yourself to improve."

Ida Rosenthal and her new husband left Russia in 1905 before he was conscripted into the Army during the czarist regime. The couple immigrated to America thinking it would be the opportunity they dreamed of. Ida became a dressmaker. To support her family, which included two children, Ida was working at her sewing machine before dawn each morning and didn't stop until after dark.

Because she put customer satisfaction first, she made one dress at a time and ensured each garment fit every customer perfectly. Her quality work soon attracted the attention of Enid Bissett, a famous boutique owner. The two formed a partnership. Ida invested almost her entire life's savings, $4,000, in the new venture. Customers began spending $125 to $300, an unheard of amount in those days, for her custom creations. Success didn't dim her innovation, however.

Rosenthal didn't like the undergarments of the time because, in her opinion, they flattened breasts, giving women a boyish look. This unnatural shape also made it difficult to ensure dresses fit properly. To solve this problem, Ida created a new undergarment which supported and enhanced a woman's natural curves. At first, it was part of the dresses she sold. Later, she joined two cups with elastic and called it the Maidenform Brassiere. By 1925, Rosenthal and Bissett focused on making brassieres exclusively.

Their goals were to produce a quality product, make Maidenform a well-known brand name, and develop a company that would survive into the next generation. They succeeded admirably and Rosenthal kept working on her goals every day until she died at 87.

Self-Confidence Based on Actual Accomplishment, Not Daydreams

> "Trailblazers do not wait for detailed instructions."

Americans are starting their own businesses at a record rate. Studies indicate 5.6 million workers over 50 have their own company; this is a 23% increase in the last 15 years. While their success remains to be seen, more people are turning to self-employment as they seek security and more control over their careers. In addition, inexpensive technology help keep costs low. One successful entrepreneur is Fanny Martin. Fanny worked up the courage to start her cookie company when she was almost 56. She had the confidence to do this after spending 30 years in large companies. Her revenues grew to $500,000 after tripling in one year.

Self-confidence is probably the most important factor involved in this big decision because:

- Specific skills are lacking.
- Startup costs are underestimated.
- Health care insurance is expensive.
- Retirement saving might be sacrificed.
- There are no paid vacations.
- Time commitments for the self-employed exceeds the amount those involved in payroll jobs expend.

Experience can sometimes be acquired quickly. Steve Simons and Russell Bane worked in the furniture industry many years before starting their own made-to-order furniture company. They were both in their mid 50s, and had many contacts who developed into customers. Most of their start-up costs were spent on a website. They now have eight employees and sales are expected to exceed one million (after three years).

Careful Analysis of Motives and Talent

> "Fate plays a part, but mostly we are what we make ourselves become."

While a teenager, Richard Sears was interested in the mail order business. He often bought products he later traded or sold. Sometimes he turned a profit. His interest led him to believe that the mark-up on watches selling for $25.00 was too high. He bought them for $12.00 and sold them for only $14.00, but made $5,000.00 (a huge amount in the 1880s) in a few months. The 23-year old took that money and started the R. W. Watch Co.

Sears moved his company to Chicago and hired a watchmaker, Alvah Roebuck. The two later formed the famous partnership everyone knows – Sears & Roebuck. Going back to his teenage experience with mail order, Sears created a mail order catalog and began selling products – everything from jewelry to buggies. In a few years, his mail order catalog had more than 500 pages!

Another teenager, Frank Woolworth, became interested in dry goods. In the late 1860s, he couldn't find work in this area so he took a bookkeeping course, thinking this would make him more attractive to employers. Eventually, he was hired by a dry goods outlet in New York. Woolworth quickly became the store's top employee and convinced the owner to become a financial backer in a new venture he called the Great 5-Cent Store. The business led to the five-and-dime concept and the successful Woolworth chain became a nationwide retail icon for many decades.

> "There are three ingredients in the good life: learning, earning, and yearning."
> – Christopher Morley, writer

William Mathias Scholl was the grandson of a shoemaker. At an early age, he learned that poorly fitting shoes caused pain. He thought he could create products that could ease foot pain and make money at the same. Scholl started as a shoe clerk and learned about customer needs first hand. At 18, he enrolled at the Illinois Medical College. While still in college, he introduced his first product: an arch support called the Foot Eazer.

Combining his knowledge, medical degree, and marketing savvy, Scholl introduced his products to the market in innovative ways. Knowing credibility would help sell his products, he dressed like a doctor to make sales calls. He used educational demonstrations and humor to make his product memorable. Nine years after he started his business, Scholl's firm had its first $1 million year. By the mid-1950s, he had hundreds of retail stores, and 15 manufacturing plants supplying product. Sales now are nearly $300 million a year.

Realistic Evaluation of Barriers

"Show Your Best Side"

Orville Redenbacker knew it would take 10 to 20 years to develop his product – and then, he'd probably have to take it to market himself. Despite the nay-sayers, the fourth son of a farmer wanted to create a special popcorn that all popped fluffier. Obsessed with popcorn since the age of 12, Redenbacher was later joined by his friend, Charlie Bowman. They experimented with over 30,000 hybrids.

Bowman and Redenbacher took their popcorn to food-product marketers, but no one was interested. Redenbacher then loaded his products into a station wagon and drove all over the Midwest. He talked on radio shows, gave demonstrations, and pestered merchandisers. Finally, Marshall Field's in Chicago gave him an order. In 1970, when Redenbacher stated selling his popcorn, Americans ate about a third of a billion pounds of popcorn. Now, we eat about 1 billion pounds.

"Luck is a dividend of sweat. The more you sweat, the luckier you get."
– Ray Kroc, McDonald's Founder

To encourage employees to do their best, Henry Ford doubled their salaries in late 1913. By 1914, the Ford Motor Company built more cars than all the other companies combined. By 1925, Ford built 10,000 autos every 24 hours.

Ford's business endeavors weren't all successful. The first two companies he headed failed, but he learned from his mistakes. He also was unafraid of analyzing his weaknesses and hiring people to compensate for his failings. By selecting good people and paying then well, Ford developed the modern internal combustion V-8 engine, the assembly line, and Model T. "I refuse to recognize that there are impossibilities," Ford once said. "I cannot discover that anyone knows enough about anything on this Earth definitely to say what is and what is not possible."

"Talent should be spent, not saved."

William Clark wanted to have a military career like his father. But life had a different plan for him. Probably best known as part of the Lewis-Clark team, Clark prepared for the expedition by studying map drawing and astronomy. The 8,000 mile trip gave him the opportunity to create 140 maps of the U.S. Territory west of the Mississippi, not including those from Indians and traders.

When he wasn't working on maps, Clark drew the plants and animals he saw over the two-year trip. Because of his attention to detail, scientists found his drawings valuable for more than 100 years. During his travels, Clark made friends with many Indian tribes. His attentiveness and notes on Indian culture, religion, and customs, helped him become trusted and respected by Indian leaders, who considered him a friend and advocate.

With these solid contacts and relationships, he became the Federal Government's chief Indian negotiator. Although the government's policy of moving Indians to reservations remains controversial, Clark believed it was the only way for Indians to save their culture and avoid war with the U.S.

Elimination of Distractions

"The first law of survival is *Respect Yourself.*"

Galileo Galilei was an honest, practical man who loved science and math. In 1624, the Pope told Galileo to write a book which would be "a truthful account of the universe." What the Pope really wanted, though, was a book that would explain the universe the way the church saw it: that everything revolved around the Earth. Because of Galileo's reputation and because the Pope was a personal friend of the family, he probably thought the book would support the church.

For nine years, Galileo worked on the project and decided to tell the truth as he saw it. He let the truth speak. His book supported Nicolas Copernicus' theory that the Earth and other planets revolved around the sun. The early 1600s were dangerous times for people to speak out against the church or notions the church wanted to advance. Offenders were brought before the Inquisition.

Because Galileo had some well-placed friends, they were able to spare him from almost certain death. Instead of being executed, he was convicted of heresy and confined to a small house under constant surveillance. While in confinement he painted, played the lute, and wrote *Two New Sciences*. This work was basic reading on motion and the properties of matter for generations of physicists, mostly notably for Isaac Newton.

Galileo introduced experimentation to the scientific community. While earlier scientists based their proofs solely on logic, Galileo added scientific experimentation to validate ideas. His inspiration and experiments led to the world's most accurate clocks, the perfection of the telescope, and many astronomical discoveries. But perhaps his greatest contribution was popularizing science by speaking and writing in language most people could understand.

"Integrity is not exercised in words, it is lived in deeds."

CHAPTER 6

Winners, Losers, and Also-Rans

A serious study of the reasons for success inevitably encounters some underlying, bedrock factors. In this chapter, we examine ten of them.

- Parental influence
- Seeking responsibility
- The pitfalls of ambition
- How stars can lose
- Solving yesterday's problems
- Recovery
- Short cuts
- Nurturing strange ideas
- Pressing forward
- Concentration

Parental Influence

"If you want to see what children can do, you must stop giving them things."
– Norman Douglas, author

Parents, grandparents, relatives, and teachers have a special opportunity to observe and influence one of life's most fascinating elements – the creation and destruction of trust. Infants are trusting because they are dependent, for food, physical needs, and emotional support. But chronological age and physical growth is no guarantee that this inherent trust will be sustained.

We are born to trust others but not necessarily to trust ourselves or to be trustworthy. The key is how and by whom we are influenced, especially in the formative stages of childhood and youth. People will lie, cheat, and steal unless they are taught to be honest and trustworthy and shown the consequences by people they respect. That reality alone is probably the greatest responsibility of adulthood.

"Heroes are not scarce. Talk to anyone whose parents loved them, sacrificed for them, and set an example of honesty, integrity, faithfulness, and hard work."

Seeking Responsibility

Some people assume responsibility wherever they encounter the opportunity. Draper Kauffman always searched for ways to help his country. Unable to serve on ships because of poor eyesight, Kaufman was also forced to drop out of the U.S. Naval Academy when it raised its sight standards from 18/20 to 20/20. Instead, he became an ambulance driver for the French army just before the German invasion.

About his decision to volunteer, he wrote his father: "I realize that my contribution is going to be small and unimportant, but I know it will be a heck of a lot easier to live with myself if I go." After his bomb-disposal abilities became known to the Navy, he was recalled to the U.S. and commissioned as a Lieutenant in the Naval Reserve He was awarded a Navy Cross in 1942 for defusing a 500-pound bomb that didn't explode near an Army barracks at Pearl Harbor.

Kaufman became the nation's first frogman and the founder of the SEALS Naval Special Warfare Units. The Navy asked him to start a new school for bomb-disposal and underwater reconnaissance. After designing the selection process and what should be taught, Kauffman received another Navy Cross for his actions during a landing at Saipan. He was always willing to lead by example and never hid behind a desk or his rank. After an eye doctor cleared him for duty, Kauffman commanded ships and served as Superintendent of the Naval Academy.

> "You promote yourself every time you take on a new responsibility."
> – William Gore, Executive

The Pitfalls of Ambition

> "Predictable, honest people tend to move ahead.
> Devious, deceptive people get caught in their own web."

Ambition does not assure success. In fact, it can become a handicap if caused by jealousy, resentment, or envy. When ambition prompts us to believe we automatically deserve what others have, we deceive ourselves. Politicians then use that notion to encourage:

- Class warfare.
- Political appeals to increase public spending for entitlements.
- Social policies which punish savers and reward non-producers.

The net result is that a small minority of producers are required to support a large majority of low-skilled, unmotivated dependents seeking ever more "free" goods and services from the government and employers.

> "Show me a man who cannot bother to do little things and I'll show you a man who cannot be trusted to do big things."
> – Lawrence Bell, aviation executive

Ambitious people fail when they:

- Select people who will not be accountable.
- Assume that everyone who opposes them is stupid.
- Neglect to set measurable goals.
- Retain people who do not perform.
- Disregard the difference between failure and mismatch.
- Withhold praise for good work.
- Bluff without facts.
- Consider opinions before facts.
- Ask the wrong questions.
- Look for *who's* wrong before *what's* wrong.
- Solve the wrong problems.
- Confuse experience or credentials with results achieved.
- Allow weaknesses to prevail over strengths.
- Fake commitment to team success.
- Ignore advice of those closest to the problem.
- Support personal relationships over performance.
- Substitute good intentions for achievement.

- Overlook the difference between activities and accomplishment.
- Favor efficiency over effectiveness.
- Tolerate and overpay mediocrity.

How Stars Can Lose

When a group of all stars refuse to work together, it doesn't matter how good individual players are – the team still loses. They lose games and they also lose respect for themselves. Take the 2004 U.S. Olympic basketball team for example.

Any Olympic team wants to have the best talent in its country. But, when individual U.S. players did not work as a team and follow the rules laid down by authorities, many problems followed. Some players ignored curfews and did not get enough rest to play their best. Individuals called attention to themselves. Egos prevailed and the team did not even qualify for the championship game.

Successful team players keep their egos in check. Those who are insecure or immature do not. In a team situation, attention seekers are a liability. Selfish people are a handicap.

> "To find the best people for big, difficult jobs, look for these qualities:
> • Restless minds • Healthy bodies
> • Relentless attitude."

Solving Yesterday's Problems

Whenever you start a new job and offer a different way to do something, someone usually says, "But that's not how we've done it before." Nothing drains the energy, motivation, or creativity of a new employee more quickly. This little caution warns the newcomer their opinion will not be not valued and the organization prefers no change. Even if it is only one person's opinion, progress slows and growth stops. No organization can solve today's problems with yesterday's solutions – the world will pass it by.

To gain and keep momentum, employees must be focused on results, not activities. They must be challenged and empowered to think. Turf wars cannot be tolerated. What worked yesterday might not work today. Or, what did not work yesterday with a little tweaking might be the right solution today. Or, some seemingly off-the-wall comment might lead to an unexpected solution. To live only for today should never be the purpose of a dynamic organization.

> "Losers try to use yesterday's answers for today's problems."

Recovery

When babies learn to walk, they stumble and fall very frequently. But, eventually, the shaky step turns into a confident walk and then a run. Adults often forget this. Progress is not instant. Recovery is a continuing challenge, be it illness, injury, or any other interruption or setback.

In her time, Helen Wills was as well known as royalty or movie stars. She was the singles winner of the Women's American Lawn Tennis Championship (now known as the U.S. Open) in 1923–25 and 1927–30. She was the women's champion at Wimbledon in 1927–30, 1932–33, 1935, and 1938. In 1928–30 and 1932, she won the French Championships.

But in 1926, she had an appendectomy which was slow to heal. Some thought she would retire. No way. She quickly began physical therapy and within a year was back winning. But again in 1933, severe back pain caused her to default an important match. Critics said the back injury was a hoax because she was losing when she stopped.

Doctors, however, explained that without surgery her back could have been ruined forever. Then, after another year of physical therapy, Wills created her special place in tennis history. She came back and won Wimbledon again.

> "Confidence grows when obligations are met. It dies when we quit."

A near-fatal car accident left Julio Iglesias partially paralyzed for two years. While recovering, he listened to the radio and wrote poems. A friend gave him a guitar to pass the time. Soon, Iglesias was putting his own songs to music. In 1968, he won a Spanish song festival award for his song "Life Goes On." It became Spain's No. 1 hit. By 1983, Iglesias had sold 100 million records in six languages. Since then, he's recorded 76 albums and sold more than 250 million copies.

No Short Cuts

Football great Otto Graham's talent started showing when he was young, but in many other ways. While in high school, he was: selected to be on the Illinois All-State basketball team; played baseball, football, and tennis; and was an accomplished cornet, French horn, piano, and violin player. No matter what Graham decided to do, he worked hard and long. His outlook – "I was born with good coordination, a gift from God. But I worked for everything else I ever got out of sports. There is no short cut to success. It takes practice."

Experts believe he was an excellent quarterback because he practiced countless hours with his receivers by watching their shoulders so he could anticipate where to throw the ball – even if the planned path was blocked or abandoned. This extra effort resulted in great precision. Graham led the Cleveland Browns to ten championship games in ten years, was named all-league quarterback nine times in ten seasons, and was inducted into the Pro Football Hall of Fame.

> "Great things are done by a series of small things brought together."
> – Vincent Van Gogh, artist

Most of us can easily daydream for a few minutes while we wait at a stoplight or take a train or bus to work, but Peter Lynch found ways to make every second count. When he carpooled into work, he read. When others might relax after a tough day on the road, he went to his hotel room to read annual reports. The manager of Fidelity's Magellan Fund ate and slept mutual funds.

Only about ten percent of the people who called got 90 seconds to talk with him. Lynch let his secretary and traders handle most of his calls. He liked to start earlier in the morning and was often disappointed when companies he was visiting couldn't get someone to meet him at 6:00 AM. By starting early, he was able to visit 40 to 50 companies a month and get the on-site knowledge he needed to make a decision.

But keep this in mind – Lynch's schedule was so demanding he did not spend much time with his wife and kids. He became exhausted and retired at 46. Pacing, too, is important.

Nurturing Strange Ideas

Many good ideas for products start with daydreaming and common situations. Take Bill Schlotter and Tom Coleman, former mail carriers. One Halloween, the two noticed that a child carrying a bright, green-glowing stick seemed entranced by it. They wondered if a lollipop on the top of a similar stick would be even more attractive. They created a prototype and sold the idea to Cap Candy. First called the Glow Pop, it was later renamed the Laser Pop. Continuing with that success, Schlotter and Coleman wondered if kids would go for a lollipop that spins automatically. While adults found the idea a little strange, kids loved it and convinced their parents to spring for the $2.99 sucker.

John Osher, who headed Cap Candy, took the little lollipop motor to the next level by adding the motor to a toothbrush. Presto! The Spinbrush, which he later sold to Proctor and Gamble for $475 million! From lollipop, to toothbrush, to about half a billion dollars. Wow.

> "Losers wait for fruits to fall.
> Winners shake the tree."

Pressing Forward

Back in 1908, automobiles were replacing horse-drawn buggies. William Hoover was, at the time, making his living selling horse collars and harnesses. He foresaw his business dwindling.

At the same time, an inventor, James Murray Spangler, had unsold inventory that was affecting his financial situation so much he took an extra job as a department store janitor. Spangler had asthma and found that cleaning the store rugs worsened his condition. Always curious, he created a machine he called the electric suction sweeper. The first product looked very strange – it combined a fan motor, pillow-case, broom handle, roller brush and metal soapbox. It sounded weird, too . . . but it worked.

Spangler believed other people would find the contraption helpful so he got a patent, but was flat broke with no way to market it. He showed the sweeper to friends, one of whom was William Hoover's wife, Susan. William quickly saw a new product that could take the place of his dying ones and bought the patent. By constantly improving and adding attachments, Hoover's vacuum cleaner became the standard for an exploding industry.

"Winners do things they don't have to do."

For most tennis players, the game changes with the competition but not for Jimmy Connors. He played hard and fast with all of his competitors all of the time. His mother, Gloria, a good tennis player herself, planned tennis careers for her sons John and Jimmy. A section of the back yard served as a tennis court. Gloria coached Jimmy during tough games. "He couldn't wait to kick the slats out of his playpen and get started in life," she once said.

Connors became famous for his all-or-nothing, full speed approach to tennis. If you made a good shot against him, you could expect that he would charge the ball and return it with speed and force . . . or die trying. Over his career, Connors won 109 singles titles (including 8 Grand Slam crowns), was ranked number one in the world for 159 straight weeks, and was one of the top ten tennis players from 1973 to 1988.

Concentration

Most adults have heard of Ella Fitzgerald. We know her creative singing and powerful voice, but few realize that she fought her own battles throughout her life. Her mother died when she was 15. She spent time in a reform school and struggled with stage fright throughout her entire career.

Though criticized severely, Ella knew singing was her life. She sang constantly – often to herself. Fascinated by band sounds, she tried to imitate the sounds of band instruments with her instrument – her voice. She often sang nonsense syllables copying the instrumental solos. She perfected legendary trumpeter/singer Louis Armstrong's "scat singing" technique and made it widely popular.

Fitzgerald was a constant learner and hard worker. She performed over illness and stage fright. She knew she needed to prepare new, modern songs to increase her audience and attract young people.

By the end of her career, this singer, whose critics said had "limited vocal and emotional range" received 13 Grammy Awards (including the 1967 Bing Crosby Lifetime Achievement Award), the Kennedy Center of Performing Arts' Medal of Honor (in 1979), and the National Medal of the Arts (in 1987).

"Ability is what you're capable of doing.
Motivation determines what you do.
Attitude determines how well you do it."
– Lou Holtz, football coach and broadcaster

No stranger to failure, Gail Borden invented a wagon that doubled as a boat. It sank. He then invented a dehydrated beef biscuit which won a gold medal at a London Exposition in 1851 but was a business failure.

Before the days of Louis Pasteur and refrigeration, people traveling by ship across the ocean were dependent on the health of the ship's cows for good quality milk. On a return trip from London, Borden saw five children die after drinking milk from a sick cow. He decided he would do something to stop this kind of death.

Combining his knowledge of dehydration with some kitchen experiments, he first tried to dehydrate milk. But cooking until the water evaporated sometimes caused it to burn. Then, after visiting friends in a Shaker colony where they condensed maple sugar using vacuum pans, Borden got another idea. He used the vacuum pans to condense his milk, cooked it slowly, and added a little sugar for preservation. He got a patent for his process and started the Borden Condensed Milk Co. The instant coffee and evaporated milk it developed were staples for U.S. military forces in both World Wars.

> Do it now. Tomorrow the opportunity may be lost.

CHAPTER 7

How Far? How Fast?

> "There are few quick fixes. Just as healing a wound takes time, so do all good changes."

It's hard to argue with the point that those who "hope for the best" and wait for it to happen are likely to lose. But the opposite conclusion is not trust worthy either. Even the most deliberate, calculated, and fine-tuned planning carries no guarantees. The three most reliable keys for venturing are *alertness, scanning,* and *starting.*

Unless we constantly think about where our interests, talents, and experiences can be applied, opportunities will fly by. Unless we take time to investigate new options, we will stagnate where we are now. Unless we accept accountability for deliverables in actual workplace situations, we will never undergo the testing required to determine whether the world wants what we have to offer.

Benefiting from this concept is determined by responses to four basic issues:

- Hold on or move on
- Here's tomorrow – how winners prepare
- Stay flexible
- Beware the hazards of ambition.

Here is why each is critical:

Hold On or Move On?

With the employment situation so tenuous these days, it's often difficult for people to decide if it's best to hold on to the position they have or to take a chance and move to another.

If you are one of these people, here are some questions to think about.

- How good are the future job opportunities here? Can I take on additional responsibilities, continue learning and advancing? Or is the future looking bad or uncertain?
- How are employees treated? Is there flexibility to adjust to employee's changing lives? Are training, educational opportunities and incentives offered?

If you decide to stay with your current firm, consider these tips:

- Keep track of your accomplishments. Keep them in a file or, better yet, update your resume with them. Be prepared for new opportunities.
- Keep learning. Find a mentor or watch people you admire.
- Build relationships. Treat everyone with respect. You never know which person will know about a new opportunity or have an inside track with a hiring manager. Peers could end up being your manager. A support staff person may be a manager's confidant.
- Be ready. Have that resume in top form. Prepare for an in-company interview in the same way you would prepare for an outside interview!
- Never cut down the competition. Instead, explain how you are different and how your experiences and skills are a good match for this opportunity.

> "If everything is under control,
> you're going too slow."
> – Mario Andretti, race car driver

Conditions Are Never Ideal

How do you go from being $75,000 in debt to earning millions? For Rosie Herman, a manicurist and mother of twin girls, it was a case of improving on a good thing. Her sister, Schura Normand, stopped by one day with some Origins salt scrub. Herman tried the product and decided she could make something similar but better. She made her own special mixture and called it "One Minute Manicure." At first, she gave her products to her friends as gifts. Then friends and others began asking for more. In just five years, Herman sold $20 million worth of the $25-a-jar scrub.

"Favorable conditions are rare. Use them all."

Knowing when to run and how far helped Bill Rodgers become a World Class Marathon competitor. He didn't run year-round or fit the commonly accepted mold. Rather, he focused on pacing himself in workouts as well as during races. Because he started when amateurs weren't allowed to make any money from running, he worked as a teacher. He ran in the mornings and after school and used vacation and sick time to compete in meets.

Rodgers has run 28 marathons in under 2 hours and 15 minutes. He was the world's number one ranked marathon runner for three years and was inducted into the Long Distance Runners Hall of Fame as well as the U.S. Track and Field Hall of Fame.

> "It is not because things are difficult that we do not dare; it is because we do not dare that they are difficult."
> – Seneca, Roman dramatist

In the 1880s, Carl Elsener was a poor, restless hat maker in Switzerland. Because Swiss culture went against the notion of mass producing items formerly made by craftsmen, Elsener created a trade association for them to produce high-quality knives for the Swiss Army. But, after his initial delivery in 1891, a German company made the knives cheaper, forcing Elsener out of business. He lost everything except his belief that he had a good idea. Elsener made an officer's version of the knife, which was lighter and had fewer tools. Learning from past mistakes, he protected the product legally and created a factory to manufacture it.

Even though the Swiss Army didn't make the knife standard issue, officers started asking for it at local stores. By upgrading his knife and appealing to new markets, especially outdoorsmen, demand for his knife increased. Today, the factory makes 34,000 knives a day.

Here's Tomorrow – How Winners Prepare

> "Look up – but not so high you cannot see what lies ahead."

Although other toy makers made fun of him as first, Ty Warner was convinced success lay in being different. He thought that filling stuffed animals with stuffing made them less life-like so he decided to use less filling. The competition thought he was being cheap.

He also did his marketing differently. Instead of going to the big chains, he sold limited quantities to gift stores. They paid their bills in a more timely fashion which improved his cash flow and gave the added benefit of making his toys seem less mass-produced and more of a collectible item. By retiring his "Beanie Babies" at their peak popularity, demand increased and the value for collectors skyrocketed.

Warner also noticed that no one was creating a quality stuffed toy for under $5.00. He saw greater demand at that price point because it would not require a child to convince a parent to part with more money. Although revenue figures for Ty Inc. remain undisclosed, Forbes listed Warner as one of the 400 richest people in America in 1999.

> "It does not matter how slowly you go as long as you do not stop."
> – Confucius, Chinese philosopher

Only a few big Internet companies have survived the .com crash. Amazon is near the top of the list. Founder Jeff Bezos believes his success is based on the fact that he carefully hired employees to create the kind of company he wanted. "Cultures aren't planned. They evolve from the early set of people," he says.

The people Bezos selected needed to be comfortable with contradictions, because he believes they should be both stubborn and flexible. Kind of like a gambler, you need to know when to hold them 'em and when to fold 'em. Bezos also believes Amazon must have employees who are first and foremost in tune with customers. Given a choice of being customer-, competitor-, or internally-focused, he wants Amazon to concentrate on customers, period!

Decisions at Amazon are first made based on fact, if facts are available. "The great thing about fact-based decisions," he contends, "is that they overrule the hierarchy. The most junior person in the company can win an argument with the most senior person with regard to a fact-based decision." If the facts are illusive, Bezos says, experiment – but rely on common sense. Keep it simple: think about what would be best for the customer.

Amazon is not the only company selling books on-line, but it does have an admirably loyal following. Customers like the little things Amazon creates – like Wish Lists and a warning system to advise customers that they have previously purchased a title. Some features may, in the short term, mean lost sales but Bezos believes what is best for the customer will turn out, over the long run, to be best for Amazon. Bezos is now worth $5 billion.

> "He who wishes to be rich in a day will be hanged in a year."
> – Leonardo de Vinci, artist, inventor, scientist

At one time, most people believed the human body could not run a mile in less than four minutes. Roger Bannister would not accept that conclusion. He wanted to break the 4-minute mile barrier and then have a medical career. He decided that the first race of the season would be his best opportunity to beat the record.

Bannister spent the winter of 1954 training strenuously. For the first time in his life, he got a coach to encourage him. Shortly before the race he filed his spikes on a grind stone at his hospital lab. Then, he rubbed graphite on each one. The weather was less than ideal. It was raining, cool, and windy. Bannister wondered if this was the right time, but when he got to the track the wind slowed down. During the lull, he started and broke the "unbeatable" record with a time of 3:59.4. After 1954, having accomplished his first goal, Bannister settled into his second. He completed his medical degree, became a neurologist, and then master of Oxford's Pembroke College.

> "Those who persist overcome.
> Those who quit come over."

For athletes, hard training and physical workouts leads to success; for others, thinking, planning, and studying the market are better predictors. King Gillette's story is right on the mark. When Gillette worked for the Baltimore Seal Company, he developed a relationship with the company's president, William Painter. Painter suggested that he think of something disposable people would use, throw away, and purchase again.

One day, while shaving, Gillette connected the dots: why not make a disposable razor! After researching the market, he discovered there had been no significant improvement for generations in the tools men used to shave. He concluded that even if his razors were superior, he could make more money selling blades than razors. With this knowledge and years of testing, Gillette designed a razor and started a company. He invested in advertising using sports figures to pitch his product. The company's future was secured in a 1903 agreement with a wholesaler, who agreed to buy 50,000 razors and 100,000 blades.

Stay Flexible

"The best leaders combine relentlessness and patience with thoughtful evaluation of options."

By age 18, George Parker had created two games and licensed a third. The games brought in some money but not as much as working as a journalist for Boston's Commercial Bulletin. After an illness, he quit the Bulletin. The paper wanted him back and offered him four times what he was making. A competing paper offered him even more. Parker was having a hard time deciding which offer to take so he asked his older brother Charles what to do. His answer – "Follow your heart."

George persuaded Charles and a third brother, Edward, to join him in forming Parker Brothers, which by 1910 became the largest game maker in the U.S. They brought games (like Ping-Pong, Tiddledy Winks, Clue, and Mah-Jongg) from overseas to America and American games (like Flinch, Rook, and Monopoly) to the rest of the world.

George liked to conceive and market games people would find educational and fun. He enjoyed creating games (such as Rook) but he wanted to expand. He acquired rights to games other people invented so he could expand more rapidly. Undoubtedly his best decision ever was acquiring "Monopoly." He decided to halt production on all other products and focus on the introduction of this new game because he believed it was a winner. As protection, Parker wisely bought the rights to a similar game and so had a "monopoly on Monopoly" (He had learned this lesson from an earlier game war). Monopoly turned a $1 million profit for the company in 1936. The Parker Brothers brand name, now owned by Hasbro Inc., has over 2,000 products.

"If you can't find an answer, don't assume there is none."

In the late 1950s, John Calamos' parents gave him all of their savings, $5,000, to invest for them. He had been investing his own meager saving and money of a few others but that responsibility to his parents was scary. The elder Calamos had immigrated to Chicago. John worked in his father's grocery store so he knew the value of money and what this savings meant to his parents. He carefully researched growth stocks and made his selection.

About this time, he realized he needed more knowledge so he took finance and economics courses. To round out his education, he took philosophy and other social sciences classes. He joined the Air Force and spent five years in the service – one in Viet Nam when he learned that "knowledge is your best bet to control risky situations."

His researching skills led him to a type of security – a convertible bond – that few people invested in.

(A convertible bond represents debt issued by companies that can be "converted" into shares of stock at any time.) In 1985, Calamos' brokerage firm (started in 1977) introduced the Calamos Convertible Fund. The Fund now manages over $1.5 billion in assets.

> "When haste decreases accuracy, slow down."

Jim Casey and his friend Claude Ryan started a messenger service when they were in their late teens. In the early 1900s, before telephones were widely used, it was a good business. Because competition was stiff, the partners decided to be available for their customers 24 hours a day, seven days a week. This gave them an edge over the competition.

After the telephone found its way into more homes, business decreased. Casey, though, found new customers and a slightly different service. He started delivering packages for department stores, orders for restaurants, and special delivery packages for the post office. He hired drivers and had the same drivers cover the same routes so they could develop rapport with their customers. Casey's business moved down the west coast and then across the country.

After World War II, the shopping habits of people changed. Malls sprang up and people shopped there, taking their packages home with them. Again, Casey's business had to change. The company, United Parcel Service, moved into the common-carrier service. UPS revenue now is over $31 billion with customers in over 200 countries.

> "Success does not come by winning every day, but by steadily advancing to a new plateau."

Necessity may be the mother of invention, but Kemmons Wilson's success had its roots in a family vacation. In the early 1950s, motels were mostly used by salesmen and casual lovers so they were not exactly nice, reputable places a family would find comfortable. Wilson, his wife, and their five children had what he called, "the most miserable vacation trip of my life."

The surprises were not pleasant. The motels were shabby and the owners liked to tag on extra charges for each of the children. When Wilson got home, he decided he would start a motel chain. Each unit would have free TV, air conditioning, and children would stay free in their parents' room. Each motel would have a swimming pool. Parents could request a free crib for their children. The rooms would be clean and reasonably priced. These were all firsts in the industry. Many thought he was dreaming. At the time, only the well-to-do or salesmen traveled. Plenty of hotels served these customers. Families just didn't travel much but Wilson thought that was going to change. And change it did with the opening of the Holiday Inn.

Beware the Hazards of Ambition

Ambition is a valuable quality because it usually points to a self-starter. But, unfortunately, it can also be almost completely self-centered. This type of "all eyes on me" person has a limited arena in which to be successful. Individual sports like golf, tennis, and swimming come to mind. But when group effectiveness is needed, ambition must be controlled. If it is not:

- Results are limited to what the person can do alone.
- Others become unmotivated to work because they know they will get no credit.
- They take precious time making sure everything focuses on them, especially microphones and video cameras.
- They maneuver outcomes that favor their personal goals – not the team's.
- They reward "suck ups" and ignore key people working in the background.
- They work hard to avoid situations where their weaknesses will become known.
- They don't engage in conflict where their image may get tarnished so we never know how strong they will be in tough times.
- They seek projects where it is easy to shift blame for failure on others.

Consider these clues to benefit most from your ambition:

- A commitment without action is an empty glass.
- A promise unkept is a debt unpaid.
- Inspect what you expect before it is too late.
- The shorter the learning time, the faster solutions can be found.
- The faintest ink is better than the finest memory. Write it down!
- Imagine your goal is a magnet. Have it pull you toward it.
- Adding new skills creates choices and avoids dead ends.
- Achievers will learn from anyone, anything, anywhere.
- A decision not to decide is a score for your opponent.
- Unfocused energy is unused power.

> "Success is hollow if the achiever is not admirable."

At first glance, David Beckham might appear to have fallen for the fast life. But appearances can be deceiving. Beckman's marriage to former Spice Girl Victoria Adams might have signaled the beginning of the fall. England's most famous soccer player and the pop singer attracted the attention of the pop-culture media. When he changed hairdos regularly and dressed flamboyantly, the media couldn't resist.

While he has the attention of the youth and media, though, he teaches them about being tolerant of minorities and is known for his charity work. London's *Guardian* wrote, "His talent is enviable and his honesty is impeccable. Beckham is more than a footballer. He represents the best of British youth."

> The difference between a job and a career is the difference between 40 and 60 hours a week."
> – Robert Frost, poet

Henry Ford had two previous business failures behind him when he tried to get backers for a third. It took a while but he finally got enough investors. They disagreed, however, on a major point. Ford wanted to produce affordable cars for the common man; the investors wanted him to create expensive cars for the wealthy so they would have a higher profit margin. Ford prevailed and bought out their stock as soon as the Ford Motor Company started making money.

By using a revolutionary assembly line, Ford was able to crank out 10,000 cars a day. Consumer prices fell from $825 in 1908 to $360 per car by 1916. The factory employed 100,000 people. Biographers seem to agree that the key to his success was his ability to make complex things simple. Ford, though, usually gave credit to his employees: "Higher wages are not an additional cost under proper management. Better-paid workmen are more willing and more efficient."

"Ambition becomes self-defeating when it discourages needed helpers."

As the baby boomers begin retiring, many U.S. firms are planning for the next generation of managers. Executives from the top 1,000 companies are grooming their successors. Succession planning is becoming more important than ever. Take Wal-Mart, for example. Two times a year, Wal-Mart leaders get together to talk about the business and possible successors. If future key players do not have a development plan, they will shortly after the meeting. Employees who show cultural, leadership, and people skills are likely candidates.

Planning for the future is vital for survival. Customers, investors, and employees all need to know that the company will survive and prosper long after the current leaders are gone.

"Be grateful for those who kindly show us how to improve."

CHAPTER 8

The Main Source of Perseverance

"Pride initiates.
Commitment continues.
Perseverance completes."

Most progress halts for internal reasons. We stop and can't get started again unless we are pulled or pushed. Why? The chief culprit, I believe, is that we haven't gained confidence in self-confrontation. We haven't learned the simple skills involved in:

- Asking and answering basic questions about how we got in trouble.
- Identifying changes we alone must make.
- Resisting the temptation to blame others for our problems.
- Committing to a step-by-step written plan.
- Enlisting trustworthy helpers.

As you find helpers, beware of those who:

- Want you to be dependent on them (like parents who don't allow their children to grow up).
- Believe you are weak and will fail without them.
- Enjoy a feeling of superiority.
- Will try to manipulate you away from your values, aims, and ambitions.

A good way to start this process is to ask, how do I describe myself? Write your answers. For example:

I believe I . . .

Positive
- am upbeat
- like tough jobs
- know what help I need
- am cooperative
- keep going

Negative
- complain a lot
- avoid responsibilities
- take credit, even if I don't deserve it
- like attention on myself
- am easily distracted

Where Responsibility Begins

The Higher Education Act, which allows the Federal government to deny aid to applicants who have been convicted of selling or possessing drugs, is controversial. Some people believe that the government should not fund or help fund the education of people who have been convicted of drug use or sale. Some believe an education is a good way to encourage people to reform. Still others believe that students who lie on the form or who use or sell drugs but have not been convicted slip through the system. No matter what you believe, the bottom line is a student who wants an education will find a way to get one. People have always had unfair advantages or unfair disadvantages. The people we admire are those who take responsibility for their life and take action.

What Is Pulling You Down?

> "The harder you work,
> the harder it is to surrender."
> – Vince Lombardi, football coach

8 Words of Warning

Win
Stay
Try
Prepare
Delay
Excuse
Quit
Lose

"The difficult, we do right away. The impossible takes slightly longer," so said Philo T. Farnsworth, whose life exemplifies his convictions. At only 13, he had a concept he would later call "television." His instructors told him his idea was impossible, but he ignored them. After building the first T.V. set, Farnsworth went on to develop an electron microscope, an infant incubator and many other innovations. In 1984 he was inducted into the National Inventors Hall of Fame.

In addition to technological challenges, Farnsworth fought and won a legal battle with The Radio Corp. of America. After refusing to sell his invention to R.C.A., they sued him, claiming he stole their ideas. Fortunately he had thoroughly documented his work with notes that were signed, dated, and witnessed, so he beat the huge corporation in the courts.

"Winners see opportunities everyone else misses."

They told her she was "no competition" because women, in the 1950s, were expected to drop out of the business world when they got married. But Patsy Sherman took that comment as a challenge. She insisted that she be given the same aptitude test as the boys because she thought she'd be a good chemist and wanted an opportunity to prove it: After getting a degree in math and chemistry, she joined 3M in St. Paul, Minnesota. Soon after, an assistant accidentally spilled Patsy's experiment involving a compound that would resist breakdown from jet fuels. The substance could not be removed from her tennis shoes. Fascinated, Sherman explored the compound's protective properties. The result – Scotchguard! She and her partner, Sam Smith, share 13 patents, and she also has an additional 3. In 2001, she was inducted into the National Inventors Hall of Fame.

> "The quickest way to conquer fear is to ignore it."

His mother wasn't demonstrative and his father didn't care for him much, so Francis Chichester's life didn't start out too well. But, matters got worse. While in one boarding school, the headmaster beat him. In another, students weren't fed adequately and many died of influenza.

He tried lots of different jobs – from shearing sheep to mining for coal and gold and even started a tree farm. Then, he bought into an aviation company and found his true love – flying. After purchasing a Gypsy Moth biplane, he became the second person to fly solo from Britain to Australia. Later, he added floats to his plane. This enabled him to fly from the Tasman Sea (New Zealand) to Australia. He was the first person to make this trip solo.

Realizing war was coming, he volunteered for the Royal Air Force, but was told that at 37 he was too old to be a fighter pilot. He became a master navigator instead and invented a sun and star compass. One allowed him to navigate during the day; the other at night.

But there was one more hurdle to face: lung cancer. Deciding against surgery, he became interested in making a solo boat race across the Atlantic. He entered the race and won – in 40½ days, shaving 16 days off the previous record. Nothing held him back.

You can't wish your way to success. You have to earn it."

Constructive Compulsion

"Character consists of what you do on the third and fourth tries."
– James Michener, author

Ever since he could remember, Alan Bean wanted to be an astronaut. But how was a boy whose family didn't have much money going to get the education he needed to compete with thousands of other applicants? At his mother's insistence, Bean took the scholastics test for a Naval Reserve Officer Training Corps. scholarship. He won, but the challenges didn't end there. He was passed over twice for the astronaut jobs he applied for but he took other assignments, worked hard, and kept a positive attitude.

Later, one of his teachers from the Navy Test Pilot School, Pete Conrad, was given the command of an Apollo mission. Because Conrad was impressed with Bean's attitude and work, he selected him as one of his crew. "In a race," Bean says, "you've got to be the fastest guy. But in most things in life, persistence counts almost as much. And persistence belongs to all of us."

> "Courage is not found. It is deliberately developed via difficult decisions."

When John Deere moved to Illinois from Vermont in 1832 to set up a blacksmith shop, he discovered farmers were having trouble in their fields. Unlike Eastern soil, the Midwest ground was denser and richer. It was excellent for the crops, but stuck to their cast-iron plows. They had to stop every few steps to scrape them.

Deere experimented with different shapes and sizes. Finally, he found a discarded saw blade made of steel. He used it as the cutting edge, then contoured the cast iron upper portion and polished it until it gleamed. It worked! It rolled over the soil without sticking. Every farmer wanted one. In 1837, Deere made one plow. By 1849, he had added employees and they made 2,136 plows. Now, the company has 43,600 employees and sales of $15.5 billion. It is the largest maker of farm equipment in the world.

Deere's success can be attributed to his obsession with customers and quality. Even when his backers wanted him to stop improving his product and concentrate on mass production (because there really wasn't much competition in those days), he refused. His response – "I will never put my name on a plow that does not have in it the best that is in me."

"Integrity does not just happen. It is painfully built until it becomes the foundation for everyday living."

Most of us don't hold onto a goal for 13 or more years, but Brian Lamb did. During the Vietnam War, he worked in the Defense Department's public relations area. He was disappointed in the media coverage and wanted to get real stories to the public. In the late 70s, cable stations offered very little original programming, so Lamb thought it would be a good venue for the kind of show he wanted to see. At first, he couldn't convince any backers that a real news show would be viable. Persistence paid off when two Columbia Cable executives decided to give him a chance and some money. In 1979, Lamb's brainstorm, C-Span, took to the airwaves.

"The difference between a hero and a coward is one step sideways."
– Gene Hackman, actor

In 1830, Charles Goodyear was considered to be a failure. After a hardware business he and his father started went bankrupt, Charles Goodyear decided to follow his instincts – creating new products. First, he designed a valve for rubber life vests. But the valve melted in the heat and cracked in the cold. Undaunted, he thought there must be some way to make rubber that would stand up to heat and cold. After experimenting for five years, he accidentally dropped some of his concoctions on a stone. It hardened. But, because the discovery was an accident, he didn't know now to recreate the success. He continued his work month after month until he found the right temperature and "cooking time" to make the best rubber.

Although Goodyear died in debt, his discovery has led to a tremendous rubber industry. "Life should not be estimated exclusively by the standard of dollars and cents," Goodyear said. "A man has cause for regrets only when he sows and no one reaps." And we are all still reaping from his persistence.

> "Integrity does not just happen. It is painfully built until it becomes the foundation for everyday living."

When Charlie Nicklaus decided golfing would help rehabilitate his injured ankle, he brought his son, Jack, along to caddie. As Jack became interested in golf, his father gave him advice on how to improve. Charlie Nicklaus also taught his son about good sportsmanship, patience, and perseverance. The elder Nicklaus wouldn't tolerate poor behavior, even from his 10-year-old son. One day the younger Nicklaus threw his clubs after a bad shot. Charlie told him unless he controlled his temper, there would be no more golf.

Nicklaus often shot more than 500 golf balls a day. His commitment to hard work, practice, and constant learning helped him have a golf career that lasted over 40 years. In 1988, the Professional Golfers Association (PGA) names him Golfer of the Century.

In addition to his professional golfing career, Nicklaus has also started a company that designs golf courses. Nicklaus Design is well known in golf circles all around the world.

Last One Standing

> "Hope does not yield achievement until accompanied by work."

Joe Dittmar and the other people in the meeting weren't sure it was necessary, but they were told to evacuate the skyscraper. The meeting was on the 105th floor. They walked down 15 floors before an open fire door gave them a glimpse of the other World Trade Center tower. The other tower, the first building hit on September 11, was engulfed in smoke and flames.

At floor 78, some of the folks decided to take the elevator. Dittmar continued walking. Somewhere between the 70th and 75th floor, he felt a tremendous shaking. The second plane hit the tower he was in.

When Dittmar reached the 35th floor, he passed the firefighters who were going up. "They were going into the bowels of hell," Dittmar said, and he could tell they knew their fate. Dittmar was on of the lucky ones – he got out alive – but he never forgets those who lost their lives on that bleak day.

> "First effort is rarely the best.
> Persistence pays."

A house full of books, supportive parents, and two inventive minds led to the discovery of human flight. Their first interest in flight was fueled by a gift their father gave them: a toy helicopter. Wilbur and Orville Wright liked to play with their toys. If they broke, the brothers would recreate them, usually finding a better design.

The two first used their abilities to start a printing business. Being self-sufficient and creative, the two created their first press from spare parts they found and from firewood. Soon, the printing business took a back seat to an interest in bicycles.

The bicycle was selling quickly in the states. The two, again following their pattern, started making their own bicycles and improving on the work of previous manufacturers. Soon, they were making their own parts.

They still were intrigued, though, by flight. Remembering the helicopter their father gave them and hearing about other people trying to fly, the brothers joined forces again. Learning from the early bicycle industry, they knew people needed to be able to control their transportation. For them, it wasn't going to be good enough to just get in the air and wonder how and if they would land. So they did a great deal of experimenting.

They built a wind tunnel so they could do testing. By studying birds in flight and how bicycles wheels reduce friction, the brothers came up with some new approaches to building and testing gliders.

On Dec. 17, 1903, after a coin toss to decide who would fly their heavier-than-air machine, Orville flew for 12 seconds. In 1905, the brothers built the first practical plane, the Wright Flyer III. After receiving a patent for their plane, the brothers started the American Wright Co. to manufacture their airplanes.

> "Simple rule for success:
> Stand and Deliver."

It might be difficult to believe that one of the most famous dancers of all was, at first, thought not to be particularly talented. The family moved to New York City so his sister Adele could find better dance teachers. One day, though, Fred put on some ballet slippers and the instructor took note. Soon, the two Austerlitz (Fred later changed his name to Astaire) children were dancing together for vaudeville theaters. After dancing together for 10 years, Fred and Adele went looking for new challenges. They found a new teacher who taught them how to change their old routines and how to create new routines.

Fred Astaire liked to experiment with new steps but also responded to the audience. When he noticed they liked something, he kept doing it. For example, Fred normally didn't speak much during his routines but when his "customers" enjoyed his dialogue, he added it to his routines. After his sister retired from dancing, Fred found a new partner, Ginger Rogers, to dance with. The two of them stared in nine movies. Fred insisted on filming their routines in one shot – no edits – no camera tricks. Although this was probably harder on the dancers, he gave the audience the sense of continuity Astaire wanted them to enjoy. These films and routines have been studied by Gene Kelly, John Travolta, Patrick Swayze, and dancers all over the world.

> " 'He who stops being better stops being good.' "
> – Oliver Cromwell, Lord Protector of England

Even though his father had been the company president, Robert Wood Johnson learned the family business from the bottom up. Johnson's early experiences kept him focused on what's important – customers, employees, managers, and stock holders, in that order. Johnson liked to research everything first hand – from future plant locations to how drug stores were marketing the product to how customers and employees felt about the company.

By taking to people, Johnson communicated to them that he cared about them and their opinions. Customers and employees alike, therefore, were committed to him for the long run. Managers in the company were not punished for making a wrong decision – as long as they didn't make the same wrong decisions again. This encouraged the managers to take the risks that would be necessary to expand the business. His philosophy of business paid off. While he was president of Johnson and Johnson, annual sales grew from $15 million to $600 million!

The Fear Factor

> "Optimism is a stimulant; it develops talent. Pessimism is a narcotic; it prevents progress."

Batters, coaches, and his teammates were afraid of his fastball that sometimes traveled 100 mph. If the ball went in the strike zone, batters would have difficulty hitting the ball. If it wasn't in the zone, no one knew where it would go. Randy Johnson had a choice – slow down the pitches so he could control them or learn how to control his fastball.

Many teams found his performance too unpredictable to add him to their team. Knowing this, Johnson continued working on his pitching. He sought out pitching guru Tom House and other top pitchers and asked for their advice. At 29, many thought Johnson's pitching days were numbered. Through hard work, constant learning, and belief in his fastball, Johnson went on to win the Cy Young Award five times, was named a Major League Baseball All Star nine times, and has a contract until he's 42!

"Down, but not out."

A very unusual accident, a 7,000 pound tree fell on Rosemarie Rossetti while she was biking. After Rossetti worked for about a year to rehabilitate her body and learn how to do things for herself in this new life, she decided she needed a car – a van to be more exact. With the help of the Ohio Bureau of Vocational Rehabilitation, she had a Dodge Grand Caravan modified so she could get into the van and drive it with her hands. Now she can continue with her previous career as a professional speaker. The subject matter has changed. Before, she spoke on horticultural topics. Today, she shares her story with businesses and nonprofit groups.

"If you want to believe,
you can believe."

Mark Banks grew up in a public housing complex. The oldest of five children, Banks was often a surrogate father for the younger children. To get money to go to college, Banks joined the service. Many family members were police officers and/or military personnel so it was a so it was a good fit for him.

Banks worked his way up to lieutenant with the police force and major in the Army. While on the police force, his assignments were in some of the roughest neighborhoods. One of his Army assignments was in Iraq. During his assignments, he had seen men killed in the line of duty but somehow he had come home unharmed. His wife, Anita Banks, thought she could relax when he returned from Iraq. Two months later, he was diagnosed with incurable cancer that had spread through his entire body. The doctors gave him less than a year to live.

Throughout Banks' life, he had been a teacher and mentor – at first for his family, and later in the Army and police force. After he learned of his disease, every Tuesday night, Banks' friends would bring food and gather at his home. "No crying is allowed," said Banks. His friends and family gathered to enjoy his last days and to learn his final lesson. "I'm still teaching my friends, my colleagues, and my family," Banks explained. "Everybody's going to die – and this is how you do it."

CHAPTER 9

Who Can I Count On?

> "A vision is not a solution.
> Visionaries need workers."

The answer to this question points inward – you can count on people who can count on you. In other words, if your reputation is questionable in terms of reliability, others will trust you less. The reason is not complicated – why should they be more responsive to you than you are to them?

No mystery there, right? But we're not talking about earth-shaking events or decisions. Ask yourself, "When was the last time I shed a sympathizing tear or shared a hug or a consoling word?" If several cases come quickly to mind, chances are others appreciate you as well.

Let honesty motivate your actions. When you promise something on a certain date, deliver on time. If you say a thing to one person and the opposite to another, no one will know whether to believe you. To build trust you must be trustworthy. To build trust with others, you must trust first.

"Me first" people not only get lonely, they don't get the support they need when "the chips are on the table." A willingness to take risks is not always driven from within. We are influenced by those who have earned our trust and confidence. We seek their guidance and count on their interpretation of what we both are seeing.

These basic questions need to be answered by those aspiring to lead.

- Who are my interpreters?
- How did they qualify?
- What is the evidence?
- How accurate are they?
- How reliable are they?
- How would I fare without them?
- Who could take their place?

> "To assess the value of listening, ask yourself – 'When was the last time I had a good idea while talking?' "

Who Are My Interpreters?

They were off to a rocky start – the coach and the player. John Wooden, basketball coach at UCLA in the 70s, and Andre McCarter, at first, didn't see eye to eye on how Andre should play the game. McCarter was used to being a star – a solo player. Coach Wooden believed in teamwork.

"Teams win because they play unselfishly, and their players have solid fundamentals," says Wooden. Many of Wooden's players learned more about life than basketball from their coach. One of them was McCarter, who called home when he was thinking about leaving UCLA. His mother told him to "Do some more thinking." While he was having a bad solo practice session, his mother's and Wooden's words haunted him. Finally, he got it.

McCarter coordinated an effort to get Wooden recognized with the Presidential Medal of Freedom. He convinced many of his teammates to write letters explaining how much the coach's philosophy meant to them and how he changed their lives. In 2003, President George W. Bush gave Coach Wooden the award.

> "Loyalty is a boomerang.
> Give it and get it."

Milton Hershey set his sights on three goals: quality products, making a good life for employees, and giving back to his community. Born in 1857, he was a fourth grade dropout, but he became a millionaire from his caramel compound by 1900. Even though he worked hard, he failed in two candy businesses. Then, an aunt put up her house as collateral and a banker who believed in him loaned the money to start again.

After learning about making chocolate at the World's Columbian Exposition in Chicago in 1893, he bought needed equipment and moved it to his factory in Pennsylvania. For six years, he made semi-sweet chocolate and added more than 100 products. Eventually, Hershey decided to concentrate on milk chocolate. He perfected and sold affordable candy bars whenever people gathered – bus stops, coffee shops, newsstands, and corner stores. Because he believed in using money to improve life for employees and others, he invested extensively in community improvements. He even started a school for orphans. It is still maintained by a trust he established in – you guessed it – Hershey, Pennsylvania.

Fine Tune Your Selection Process

"The lower the expectation, the weaker the team."

Selecting New Employees

PROBLEM: Your employees don't seem to be the caliber you need to run your business effectively. They are incapable, uncommunicative, hard to lead or otherwise disruptive to the company's workflow.

DIAGNOSIS: This problem could have two causes: 1) your selection process needs to be changed; or 2) you and/or your senior staff are not doing your part to draw the best effort from employees.

PRESCRIPTION: Concentrate on the way you screen, select, and hire. Examine these ways to improve the process:

- Prepare yourself for interviews by studying candidates' qualifications in advance.
- Before the interview, prepare a list of questions.
- Know what the job requires.
- Ask open-ended questions.
- Allow the candidate to do most of the talking.
- Keep the interview flowing by using questions and statements such as:
  - Why?
  - Then what did you do?
  - Tell me some more about that.
- Give your full attention. Take only essential notes to help you remember names, dates and facts.
- Focus on the interview. Do not let the conversation drift to mutual acquaintances, common experiences, travels, hobbies, or other interesting but unimportant factors.
- Watch for signs of maturity and accountability. Does the candidate accept responsibility for decisions, achievements and mistakes?

- Probe for self-evaluations.
  - Why did you leave (or are you thinking of leaving) your last job?
  - What did you like best about your last job?
  - If you could have made changes on your last job, what would they have been? Why?
  - What was your most interesting assignment?
  - Who was the best person you ever worked for, worked with or had working for you, and why?
  - What types of people annoy you most?
  - What would you like to be doing five years from now?
  - What is most important to you: the money or the type of work you will be doing?
  - How would you describe yourself?
  - What motivates you to put forth your best effort?
  - If you were hiring a person for this position, what qualities would you be looking for?
- Watch out for braggarts.
- Check the candidate's references carefully.
- Don't make quick decisions.
- Weigh the candidate's potential in three categories:
  - Job aptitude.
  - Work attitude.
  - Ability to fit in with co-workers.

Do You Have the Help You Need?

> "When hiring, don't expect miracles from people who have only been mediocre before."

This question is bigger than it seems at first. Yes, you need hands to share in the effort, but you also need to engage the entire person. The best way for Shelly Lazarus, Chairman of Ogilvy Ad Agency to find the right people for her team, she says, is to look for open-minded people who can disagree without taking disagreements to heart. She also looks for an optimistic, can-do attitude. After the team is assembled, she gives them the mission and the freedom to achieve it. By believing in the people she hires, she can take a back seat while they implement the tasks for a successful outcome.

When her people need her, she is available. Once, after the agency lost an account Lazarus had help build, David Ogilvy asked her how she felt. He said something Lazarus still remembers and passes on to her people: "I don't care (about the financial impact). I want to know how you are because if you feel discouraged and dispirited, then Ogilvy would be weakened by what happened. If people still feel optimistic and committed to moving forward, then we are strong." Ogilvy is ranked, by *Advertising Age* as the world's number 10 agency. In 2003, revenues topped $700 million. By the way, within a year, Lazarus got the account back.

"All achievers have helpers."

Lewis and Clark's names are rarely separated, but the two men were about as different as they could be. Lewis was introverted, Clark extroverted. Lewis loved studying the stars and figuring out where they were, by using longitude and latitude coordinates. Clark loved water and plotting the course up a river. The different styles worked well for their expedition because their maps were unusually accurate for the time.

The two men openly discussed their differences and used varying points of view to strengthen their decisions. They played devil's advocate for each other. Their relationship was a strategic alliance. When they presented their ideas in public, the two had ironed out their differences and shared a common resolve. Their contribution to opening up our country is unequaled.

"I not only use all the brains I have, but all I can borrow."
– Woodrow Wilson, 28th U.S. President

Are Customers Well Served?

These days, we hear a great deal about corporate restructuring and lay offs. Those involved are told not to take it personally. That's hard to do for most of us, but two Handy Dan employees used their dismissal as a sign they should start their own business. Arthur Bank and Bernie Marcus shared views different from their previous employer. Customer service and relationship building, the two thought, were the keys to business success. An investor agreed.

Starting in 1979, Bank and Marcus opened three stores in Atlanta. They didn't understand why they were losing money, so they asked their customers and suppliers for ways they could improve. Customers said they wanted knowledgeable, enthusiastic people to help them – so that's what they gave them. To retain their customers and the people who served them best, the team realized the company had to treat people respectfully and look to build long-term relationships; not just short term profits.

Their philosophy gets results. Home Depot is the second largest retailer in the U.S. It has 1,788 stores and quarterly earnings of $1.5 billion. The approach Home Depot took during the recent hurricane season is a perfect example. Before the storms hit, people needed low-margin items and wanted stores open around the clock everyday. Home Depot did this and moved stock to the affected areas by tracking the weather.

Smart thinking. Good short-term results. Great long-term benefits.

"When the only priority is money, teamwork dies."

From the first shoe store in 1901 to the large, respected retail chain we now know, Nordstrom's has been committed to its customer's total satisfaction and shopping experience. John W. Nordstrom and his partner, Carl Wallin had built a solid reputation for customer service, selection, and quality stock. In 1928 two of John W.'s sons, Elmer and Everett, bought the store. Then, a third brother, Lloyd, joined them. The brothers believed their commitment to the customers and open communication style would spur their growth.

In 1963, the Nordstrom brothers bought a Seattle apparel store and merged it with their shoe store. By 1973, they had over $100 million in sales. Today, sales pass $6 billion and Nordstrom's has an enviable reputation in 27 states.

"Everyone in a group may have ability but it will not become a *team* unless and until there is mutual respect."

Nurturing Self-Motivation

Most of us believe that searching for a needle in a haystack is futile. How then, do medical researchers stay motivated while they probe year after year into the unknown? Before the 1600s, medical theory held that arteries pumped blood through the body. William Harvey decided to prove this wrong. After 16 years of study, his theory that the heart pumps blood was accepted. Consider also Selman Waksman: He searched through trillions of microbes that live in dirt to find one he believed would cure Tuberculosis. In that long, laborious process, he also discovered many other antibiotics.

Sometimes joining forces both helps keep people motivated and yields a better result than the sum of two parts. For example, Andrea Vesalius wanted to create a detailed textbook on the human body and wanted pictures included, but had no artistic talent. Networking led him to a master painter, Titian. The two created *On the Fabric of the Human Body*, a great work of artistic talent and medical knowledge.

Who Helps Who?

> "The Higher up you go in an organization, the more you need to let other people be winners, not just yourself."
> – Marshall, Goldsmith, Executive Coach

Think about it. When you need help at work, who do you call? Obviously, you look for someone with knowledge you don't have. But, you also think about future interaction. Most of us contact the person who is patient and supportive, as well as knowledgeable. If you want to build bridges, you must help others if you expect them to help you. If you are the type of person who has knowledge but people are afraid to talk to you, you can expect isolation or maybe even sabotage.

The old model of leadership is an authoritative one. Some people may like being told exactly what to do because it's easier for them – they don't have to think. But when that happens, they become seriously restricted. "When leaders acknowledge what they don't know," says Diana Chapman Walsh, president, of Wellesley College, "others are more inclined to share their ideas and knowledge." Just like a parent who must teach children to function independently, a good leader encourages everyone to think, give and take ideas, and grow. You can get more done when you trust people by delegating.

Walsh even suggests that if you do know the solution to a problem an employee finds challenging, you refrain from quickly giving advice. She recommends encouraging them to work through the problem until they discover a solution themselves.

"All achievers have helpers."

David McConnell realized he needed every salesperson to help him if his business, the California Perfume Co., was to succeed. To help his mostly female workforce, he developed a newsletter which detailed product information and sales tips.

He also started a correspondence department where employees could ask questions or make suggestions. It proved to be a great source of ideas for new products, marketing techniques, and process improvements. To make the products easier to sell, he stressed quality and monitored it constantly. Oh yes, you should also know that the company is now called Avon Products, and has $6 billion in sales annually.

"Fear is a motivator for some.
Success is a motivator for all."

CHAPTER 10

The Best Bet

"Most of the work we do to prepare for success is invisible to anyone else."

Last Sunday I asked myself a question which has been on my mind a long time –

"Why can't I see myself more realistically?"

Amazingly, the answer came quickly and was simple but startling. I was standing in front of a mirror. That's it! That's me! My mind raced with reasons:

- My mirror is always there.
- My mirror is always the same.
- My mirror is not biased.
- My mirror has no reason to lie.
- My mirror doesn't confuse me with back talk.
- My mirror is accurate – no one changes it to suit their purposes.
- My mirror doesn't care how I feel.
- My mirror doesn't listen to excuses or rationalizing.

- My mirror only reflects – it does not interpret what it sees.
- My mirror didn't install itself – I wanted it.

Lesson: I must interpret and decide what to do about what I see. Only I can do this and when I don't, I have only myself to blame.

- When I didn't try to anticipate a consequence and bad things happened, I must be my own mirror.
- When I trusted someone who has disappointed me before, I must be my own mirror.
- When I failed to break a bad habit, I must be my own mirror.
- When family, friends, and associates only tell me what they think I want to hear, I must be my own mirror.
- When I fall behind because I haven't developed new skills, I must be my own mirror.
- When I criticize someone for not doing something I have not done, or could not do, I must be my own mirror.
- When I promise something and don't deliver it, I must be my own mirror.
- When I let someone else meet my responsibilities, I must be my own mirror.
- If I complain about overwork but waste time, I must be my own mirror.

- If I don't know the difference between trivia and priorities, I must be my own mirror.
- If I am usually bypassed for advancement, I must be my own mirror.
- If team members rarely count on me, I must be my own mirror.

> "Goodness exists not in the outward things we do, but in the inward things we are."
> – Edwin Hubbell Chapin,
> clergyman, author

Decision Rating Guide

Use this chart to rate yourself in ten basic areas required to be an effective and objective decision maker. Place a check mark under the column (Usually, Sometimes, or Rarely) that best describes your behavior during decision-making time:

When I Approach Decisions, I . . .
(U=Usually, S=Sometimes, R=Rarely)

1. Examine as many pertinent factors as possible. ❑U ❑S ❑R
2. Require opinions to be supported by evidence. ❑U ❑S ❑R
3. Focus on ethical and moral context. ❑U ❑S ❑R
4. Analyze opponents' positions thoroughly. ❑U ❑S ❑R
5. Screen out emotional arguments. ❑U ❑S ❑R
6. Generate options objectively. ❑U ❑S ❑R
7. Consult experts without giving them authority. ❑U ❑S ❑R
8. Gather information from those closest to the problem. ❑U ❑S ❑R
9. Resist the temptation to punish those who disagree. ❑U ❑S ❑R
10. Evaluate future implications. ❑U ❑S ❑R

Give yourself 5 points for each check mark in the *Usually* column, 3 for each mark in the *Sometimes* column, and 2 for each mark in the *Rarely* column.

If you scored between	Then
40–50 points	Your decisions pass the test of time.
30–40 points	Most people will have confidence in your decisions.
20–30 points	Your decisions tend to be unreliable.

"Anyone can be a retroactive genius."

Do the Right Thing

Effective leaders must be trustworthy and honest as well as make good decisions. Vince Lombardi, a Hall of Fame football coach, knew this. He was demanding – players could not use the weather as an excuse for missing an assignment – but they respected him. The unspoken deal he struck was he would prepare them for the game during practices, but they would be responsible for the outcome. If there was no respect, they would have no confidence that advice during practices should be followed during the game – plus, they wouldn't have had the belief in themselves to think for themselves. By getting team members to think and take responsibility for their actions, he prepared them for life after football as well. Once, early in his coaching career, he kept his own brother out of a game for violating a curfew rule. He did the right thing even though it was hard.

"The joy of success is the magnet pulling us as we keep trying."

Ground Rules for Cooperation

- Groups that are involved in their own planning are generally more effective than those given a preset plan of action.
- Individuals who are systematically encouraged and assisted in setting their own levels of achievement do significantly better than those who are not.
- Groups and individuals perform better and reach planned objectives more quickly when they are provided with reliable and objective information on their progress.
- Use of carefully structured rewards will provide motivation for improvement at all levels of performance.
- Specialists within an organization may do an excellent job as measured by the standards of their own fields but still fail to contribute to achievement of over-all objectives.

"Everything that irritates us about others can lead us to a better understanding of ourselves."
– Carl Jung, psychologist

Finding the Cutting Edge

Experience as a consultant for a wide variety of organizations in many fields over many years has convinced me that these qualities are essential to develop and maintain excellence:

- An open culture. An environment where communications up, down, and across takes place as a matter of course.
- Strong shared values. The unifying element is a strong sense of commitment and sacrifice throughout the managerial ranks of the organization.
- A customer/client driven focus. Excellent organizations constantly orient themselves around their customers. Evidence is easy to see everyday.
- Willingness to invest the required funds and management time to prevent obsolescence.
- Strong and consistent leadership. Leaders understand they must provide vision for the future – not just today.
- Investment in training and career development to prevent inbreeding and provide a way to grow talent from within.
- A performance-based management system to link planning with actual results achieved.
- A compensation plan based on pay-for-performance.

Why Performance-Based Management?

"Winners know what they don't know.
Losers pretend to know but don't."

To be effective over time, organizations need:

- A planning process that clarifies assumptions and identifies overall strategic and operational objectives.
- A management system for determining priorities, setting goals, detailing action plans and evaluating progress.
- Managers who understand themselves and the key people they work with.
- A commitment to, and method for, *monitoring performance continuously* to assure that achievements are, in fact, directly related to overall objectives and rewarded accordingly.

As organizations grow, they must be certain that:

- Managers have a systematic method to relate their actions to the achievement of overall organizational goals.
- Personal responsibilities are recorded as commitments in terms of Objectives and Action Plans.

They Ventured – We Gained

"There is no comparison between that which is lost by not succeeding and that which is lost by not trying."
– Francis Bacon, philosopher

The cell phone was first invented in the late 60s/ early 70s, right? Wrong, actually D.H. Ring thought of a mobile telephone service back in 1947. But by limiting the frequencies available, the Federal Communications Commission killed the idea. It wasn't until 1968 that the FCC reconsidered its ruling.

Another Bell Labs innovation in 1947, the transistor, revolutionized the electronics industry. Created after a discovery by John Bardeen and Walter Brattain, it eventually led to the replacement of vacuum tubes and mechanical relays. Bardeen, Brattain, and their manager, William Shockley, received a Nobel Prize for Physics in 1956.

"The world will always need two kinds of people – creators to invent new things and convincers to persuade people to buy them."

A melting chocolate bar led Percy L. Spencer to think about using an active magnetron tube for an entirely different purpose. The tube he was standing near was usually thought of, in those days, as the base of the short-wave radar system. Instead of being annoyed, Spencer wondered if this tube, which was melting his candy bar, could cook anything. He dropped a few kernels of corn on it and they popped. Raytheon, his employer, introduced the first microwave oven, the Radarange, two years later. In 1967, the company introduced a commercial product.

> "Winners don't count on lightning; they bring matches."

Back in the early 1950s, drug companies weren't interested in Katherine McCormick and Margaret Sanger's idea to create a pill to prevent pregnancy. Fortunately, McCormick, heir to the International Harvester fortune, was not willing to give up. She and Sanger funded Gregory Pincus, a biologist, to do some research. The Pincus team developed a pill which prevented ovulation, and thereby, pregnancy. In 1960, the Federal Drug Agency approved it. By 1962, 1.2 million were taking the pill. Today, over 16 million American women use it as the most popular birth control method.

When he accidentally put the wrong resistor into a unit that monitored heart sounds, Wilson Greatbatch noticed it gave off a pulse much like a heartbeat. After researching the discovery and perfecting a design, he built a working model in a barn behind his house. He tested what he called his "pacemaker" in a dog, and later humans. Today, thousands believe it keeps them alive.

"Winners have two traits in common:
- They never stop asking questions.
- They never stop looking for better answers."

In 1958, Gordon Gould received a patent for the laser. At first, it was used for manufacturing purposes – cutting materials and boring holes. Building on Gould's discovery, a Bell Labs researcher, Kuman Patel, invented the dioxide laser, which led to the tools surgeons now use to perform delicate surgery. Much less invasive for the patient, hospital stays are decreased and the costs are drastically reduced.

A Look Ahead

Perhaps the greatest improvements in productivity in the 21st century are due to computers and the internet. Millions of opportunities are being created for those who are willing to embrace change. Internet and web stores give small businesses the chance to compete with giant corporations. Shoshana Zuboff and Jim Maxmin, in their book *The Support Economy,* envision a world in which a consumer makes one phone call to a personal consumer advocate who will research and recommend the product or services they need. Imagine, someone to fight your insurance battles – someone to tell you which computer or car to purchase – someone to give you career advice. Too expensive? Zuboff and Maxmin don't think so. They imagine a federation of corporations which will make this affordable for almost everyone.

> "You cannot change what's over, so learn from it."

The best way to gain confidence for venturing is to realize that the single greatest cause of failure is giving up too soon. I will be amply rewarded if this book helps you keep going.

Index